WHEN
HURT
chooses
YOU

D1452447

ANNETTE TOMLINSON

When Hurt Chooses You

By Annette Tomlinson

ISBN: 9781698666969

Copyright © 2019

Edited by: Cindy Moore with Pam Eddings

Cover Design: Terri Anderson, Annette Tomlinson, Jessica Johnson, Deanna Knight

For information, to schedule speaking events, or to order books by Annette Tomlinson, please communicate by email to:

annettetomlinson@mansionkids.org

Printed in USA

Dedication

To my husband Robert:

You are the reason I'm able to write this book. Thank you for always supporting me, believing in me and taking up the slack when my type A personality kicks in gear. You're a treasure in my life. I love you forever.

To my children:

Teresa,

Truly, you're a gift from God. It has been a joy to watch you grow in Christ, learn to pray and exemplify His Word. I count you not only as my daughter, but as a friend.

Landon,

My precious son, you've brought me great joy all the years of your life. You model Christianity in all that you do and say. God has called you to greatness. I'm proud of you.

Alayna:

You hold your mother's heart. You're the center of my world. Your laughter lights up our home. You are a leader, and God has great plans for your future.

A Tribute From My Oldest Daughter, Teresa Tomlinson-Hall

This book was written by the most powerful lady I know. Her life has taught me that my past does not define my future. My dreams will become reality. God uses people who are broken and willing to learn. Prayer is the road to healing. Forgiveness is always a must. Love is not a feeling. Love is a daily decision.

Since you have become my Mom, I have watched you fall and get back up through prayer. When you thought you looked weak, in my eyes you were strong. You have taught me to fight and never settle. That gives me strength in raising Jaicelyn. You are the reason I will fight and believe in her, because you fought for me. My children have a praying grandmother who will move mountains through prayer for them, because you have for me. I'm so honored to call you my mom.

Teresa, Brannon & their children

Acknowledgements

To my sister, Wendy Villarreal:

Thank you for protecting me, loving me, and opening your home to me when I needed a bed where I could sleep.

To my sister, Vicky Rorer:

Thank you for fighting for me as a child, and, for modeling what it is not only to follow Christ, but to truly know Him.

To Jason Watts, "The Chocolate Milkshake Drinker":

Thank you for inviting me to church and becoming my closest friend through the greatest transformation of my life.

To Canaan Apostolic UPC saints of 1988:

Thank you for loving a broken teenage girl in need of Christ.

To the students and staff of Gateway College of Evangelism:

Thank you for equipping my calling.

To Pastor Stephen and Erma Judd and my Tupelo Children's Mansion Family:

Thank you for appointing the called and allowing me to grow.

Table of Contents

Dedication 3

A Tribute From My Oldest Daughter, Teresa Tomlinson-Hall........... 4

Acknowledgements 5

Foreword by Mickey Mangun.. 9

Preface.. 10

Introduction 12

Part 1 How Hurt Chose Me 15

My Parents.. 16

The Summer of 1971 20

My Siblings 24

Crab Legs and Quarters... 26

Big Money and the Boogeyman.. 29

Our Best Years 31

Leaving Clayton 34

Mom's Rage 40

In the Kitchen 42

Raising Ourselves.. 43

Homeless and Hungry 45

Country Life 51

Two Sisters Work Together 53

Back to the Country.. 55

The Texas Cowboy.. 56

City Streets 58

Cross-Country and Track 61

My Visit to the Happy People's Church 64

Entering the Real Race 70

Hurt Chose Me Again.. 73

Quizzing 77

College Years 80

Finding my Mission Field 90

Deciding to Love 94

Part 2 My Answers to Hurt... 103

Mentors in my Life.. 104

Building a Team 111

Plugging into the Light Source... 117

When the Light Goes Out.. 118

Pushing Away from the Table... 121

Seek ye First His Kingdom 124

Forgiveness.. 126

Time, Talent, and Treasure... 130

Believing in His Promises 132

Miracles 134

Standing in the Gap 140

Living the Word 143

Painters of Light 146

It's for Me, and It's for You 152

Letter from Mom 161

My Heartfelt Prayer.. 164

Conclusion... 166

Tupelo Children's Mansion From Behind My Lens 170

To win the fight, you've got to have the right strategy and the right resources because victories don't come by accident.
From the War Room

Foreword by Mickey Mangun

Describe Annette?

Ok.

Space enough?

Warm. Welcoming. Engaging. Present. Available. Energetic. Talented. Captivating. Happy. Everywhere. Helpful. Diligent. Scattered. Loving. FUN. Giving. Encouraging. Kind. Compassionate...

If I was forced though, to sum her up in one word....I guess it would have to be *Heart*.

Nettie's got *Heart*!!!

Without doubt, one of the most amazing hearts I've ever been privileged to know.

Who would ever know that this girl, with this incredible *Heart* for God and people, is the product of a life story of immeasurable heartbreak? *When Hurt Chooses You* chronicles the life of one girl and the gracious God who redeemed her. It is a story of overcoming obstacles that would have stopped others dead in their tracks. Ultimately, it is a story of the power of God's love and grace - and how it continues to flow through my precious friend, Annette.

She has lived the words of the Old Testament's Joseph, "...what the enemy meant for evil, God has made good."

Thank you, Annette for finding the strength to put this gift in our hands.

I wish I could, with your own well-worn camera catch the expressions of everyone who reads its pages.

Preface

The words you will read in this book come from several sources, but it is my story, so it mostly comes from me. However, many of the details were told to me by my father, Fred. I spent numerous hours on the phone with him, and in the last few months of his life, I spent days beside him in the hospital, walking down memory lane. As you read this book, it might surprise you that I am able to share so candidly. My dad said that our testimonies are a combination of tests we endured and the victories of coming through them. Like me, he believed in God's forgiveness and mercy, and he was willing to admit his mistakes. Other family members who helped me share my story include, but are not limited to, my Aunt Bobbie, my step-mother, Miriam, and my two older sisters, Wendy and Vicky.

This book would not exist were it not for several people who gave me a chance, poured encouragement into my life, or told me that I could do this. First of all, thank you Cindy Hart and Kala Martin, for taking a chance on me, having me speak at Oklahoma Ladies Conference. You did not give me a topic, but both of you later said you had prayed that I would share my testimony. You did not even know what my testimony was at the time, but felt it was a story that needed to be told. In the pages of this book, it will be. Your faith ignited the fire.

About that same time, my friends, Annette George and Michelle Pace, invited me to attend the Mississippi Writers Conference. It was a two-day event and while there, I met some key players. Thank you, Kathy Lee, for encouraging me, pushing me forward to write. You said that writing was a calling and one I had to pursue. Your life and leadership give me confidence. While there, I also met Cindy Moore. Cindy, you are a passionate soul with a love for editing. I didn't realize it at the time, but God ordained our paths to one day reunite. You are a gift to me. You contacted me at a time when I wondered if I would see this book to completion, and not only forged me ahead, but also edited this book in less than two weeks. Thank you, my friend. I am honored to know you. You have taught me much. By hooking up with Cindy, I have also become friends with her mentor and partner, Pam Eddings, who is also the author of six books. Pam, you have encouraged and guided me further in the publishing process. I believe God orchestrated my attendance at this event.

Thank you my friends, Michelle Pace and Jennifer Lawrence, for being with me in the early stages of this book. Reading chapters. Meeting with me in coffee shops. Staying up late to add input and direction. You spoke into my life many times and I am grateful. I also want to thank Terri Anderson and Jessica Johnson. You helped me with the cover. Yes, Terri, you rejected about 25 of my ideas for a title until this one, the one I believe God gave me. You have always been that way. You and Jessica spent an entire day painting puzzle pieces and designing the cover of this book. I also want to thank Deanna Knight for finishing the design with the correct fonts and word placement. You are incredible my friend. I love you!

Lastly, but certainly not least, I want to thank my Aunt Bobbie, my late father, my step-mother, Miriam, and my sisters, Vicky and Wendy, for giving me hours of their time, providing me with correct facts and helping me keep dates straight. Our story has not been an easy one to tell, but each of you knew that it needed to be said. It is too powerful to be kept quiet.

Introduction

For many years I felt compelled to share my story, to give the redemptive account as to how my life's series of circumstances made me who I am today. I had never planned to get too deep. My intent was to brush lightly over the highlights I enjoyed. However, as I began to pen, suppressed memories pushed to the forefront of my mind, and I suddenly felt the urge to forge ahead and write more than I had originally planned. As I reflected on my younger years, I realized that even as a child, I possessed an optimistic personality. I tried to find the best in people and held tightly to the hope that there truly was goodness in them. I believed that tomorrow would bring better days and that I could talk myself into not being afraid, even if it meant rocking myself to sleep with thoughts of a happy song or positive story I'd heard in the past. I reached high when searching for a new friend and oftentimes pretended that I was living their life instead of my own. It was all merely a fairy tale, but at times, that fairytale dream of what could be carried me through difficult times.

When children are born, they are in need of shelter, food, nurture and love, and quite particularly in that order. These are necessities, many of which I longed for my entire childhood. I knew most families weren't perfect. I had been around enough families to come to that realization. But, even with a list of flaws, I wanted what I visualized as a family, to call my own. I longed for a stable place to live, and I desired a room without a boogey man who sometimes visited in the night. I wanted to be a normal kid with normal problems, even if those difficulties included fussing, financial struggles, and an occasional trek across country for a parent's job change or because an aging relative needed help. My aspirations were simple, but seldom met. My world revolved around instability, random and continual abuse, a longing for acceptance, and a tireless fight for survival.

To the person whose childhood was less than ideal, my prayer is that you find hope for healing in the pages of this book. Whether you already love God or have never met Him as your Lord and Savior, please embark upon this journey with me as I share pieces of my heart through the hurts and healing that came my way.

For the one who was raised on a church pew or at least knew what it was to have moral parents, please keep reading. You may have been blessed with an ideal childhood but desire a greater understanding of those of us who grew up in a world much different than your own. My prayer is that this book will serve as a light to all who read it. Whether you're among the broken, the restored, or the whole, there is something here for you. Now come along with me, as there is much to share!

Annette Tomlinson

Most of the time, a kid doesn't think about
what he's doing or why.
This is the privilege of childhood.
Robert Fulghum

Part 1

How Hurt Chose Me

To Hurt is as Human as to Breathe
J.K. Rowling

My Parents

My mom, born on January 20, 1945, in Jamesville, Wisconsin, was eleven months old when her parents divorced. At the time, she was child number four, although her mother later bore three more children. At first, my grandfather attempted to raise Mom, but he later placed her in the custody of her Aunt Gladys until age seven. From there, she was placed at Hillcrest Children's Home in Hot Springs, Arkansas. She had great memories of that home, but was only there about a year before her father came to get her. At the age of ten, Mom was placed in foster care and lived with her foster parents until the age of eighteen. A year later, Mom became pregnant with my sister Wendy, and from that moment on, her life began to spiral out of control.

My father was a merchant seaman who sailed on freighter ships all over the world. In 1966, he was taken off the ship for reckless behavior somewhere in California. Unemployed and unsure of where to go, he used his last bit of cash to get to Chicago and find work under the direction of his sister and brother-in-law.

Dad's sister was the maître d', and his brother-in-law was the Executive Chef at the Abbey Resort. They quickly taught him all they knew about the business. Dad was eager to learn. His zest for life and lust for success soon landed him the title of Executive Chef. He loved to cook and was a great leader.

The Abbey had just opened, and its goal was to create an atmosphere reminiscent to guest quarters in a "luxury, yet simple country estate." The wealthy came there to eat, to play and to be pampered at the on-location spa.

Mom's plan was to make enough money to settle down and be the mother her daughter, Wendy, needed. She was working at the Abbey as a waitress when she first laid eyes on Dad. He was a six-foot-two, big-shot chef, whose good looks and candid charm instantly swept her off her feet. She could not see through his dangerous ways. His showcase of charisma, power and strength won both the affection of women and the approval of men. He was a fast-moving, sweet-talking con artist who would one day take more than she ever imagined, without her having a choice in the matter. She was in love at all costs. It was the 1960s, and she was a Jackie Kennedy glamour girl *wannabe* during the birth of a sexual revolution. She would soon take "sowing her wild oats" to all-time new levels as this burly sailor, who stood over a foot taller than her, swept her in like a tide rushing to shore.

To those who did not know any better, Mom looked like your everyday June Carter, and Dad was her Johnny Cash. However, their jobs as chef and waitress would soon change.

Dad was raised in a godly home with good parents. They lived a simple life, with little extra. Though he had an excellent father, Dad became close friends with a man named Willis, who became his mentor. Dad idolized Willis. He was sharp-dressed, drove nice cars, had access to many beautiful women, and sported a fat bank account. His lifestyle looked fascinating to Dad, and he wanted to know all about it. Willis told Dad that to achieve his status, you first had to find a woman who was easy prey. Mom was his first victim. The object was to wine and dine her, causing her not only to fall in love with him, but also to become completely dependent upon him. And this worked.

After months of dating, Dad booked a flight for Mom to Miami. He told her that he wanted to treat her to a first class vacation at a gorgeous resort. She was excited. Moments before she boarded the plane, he said, "Gina, a nice man will be meeting you with a limousine. Go, and have the time of your life, make sure you charge well, and bring home some good money for me." She boarded the plane and flew from Wisconsin to Florida. She left a free woman, but returned home as his personal property. She no longer had a free will. She no longer had the ability to make her own choices. She was now a prostitute, and he was her pimp. Dad knew Mom struggled to stay faithful, so he used this to his advantage and contributed to her promiscuity through the world of prostitution. She admitted that she never wanted this lifestyle, but for her, it was permissible for the sake of love.

Dad knew a guy who owned a nice truck stop in Lake City, Florida, and he was happy to employ her full-time. Mom both loved and feared Dad. She couldn't live without him, and he pitched this "job" to her as a good thing. He explained to me, "I really saw no other choice in the matter. She was drop-dead gorgeous, and I knew she would become a professional fast. This made sense. We needed the money. If I didn't put her to work, I knew I would eventually lose her to someone else, so I taught her how to make fast cash doing what she did best. We lived a high-end lifestyle and needed the cash flow to get and keep the things we wanted; this was our ticket. She would work the truck stop all day. The owner got half of the money, and we got the other half. Those *johns* were nothing more than a paycheck. With each passing day, she was learning the power she held as a woman. I knew it brought her sadness at times, but she was too good at this to quit. No college degree or high-end job on Wall Street could bring us this kind of income. Our lives were set."

After a few years of working the Florida gig, Dad sent Mom to North Carolina. He had a connection there, so Mom traveled back and forth establishing many regular clients in both states. Many men desired Mom and made visits with her a regular part of their lives. She was an escape from reality for them, and they were her bread and butter. Like any *good* employee, Mom was moving up the ranks. As she improved and became more skilled at her work, her confidence level soared.

Mom always struggled with crossing the lines by allowing her clients to fall in love with her. Dad said, "She blurred the lines of business, and I couldn't trust her anymore." Because of this, there was a war that waged all my life as to whether I was my father's child or a baby born out of prostitution. Mom swore on the fact that I was Dad's child, but out of anger toward him, she didn't put his last name on my birth certificate.

The Summer of 1971

At the time of my birth, Mom was a striking twenty-six-year-old who was every bit of beautiful. Her 5'2" petite frame exhibited a sculpted figure, her head topped with a towering, toffee brown, seventies hairdo. Her eyes sparkled against her clear and vibrant, olive-colored skin. She wore a smile as large as life, which masked the recesses of her mind where secrets and sadness were stored.

I was born on a warm July day in 1971 just southwest of the Appalachian Mountains, also known as Chapel Hill, North Carolina. Annette Marie was the name Mom carefully selected in honor of her best friend, who was also her only sister.

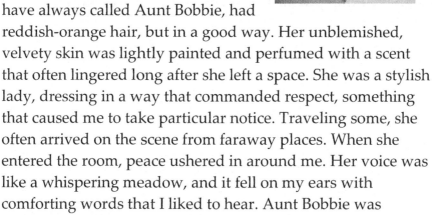

My Aunt Barbara Annette, who we have always called Aunt Bobbie, had reddish-orange hair, but in a good way. Her unblemished, velvety skin was lightly painted and perfumed with a scent that often lingered long after she left a space. She was a stylish lady, dressing in a way that commanded respect, something that caused me to take particular notice. Traveling some, she often arrived on the scene from faraway places. When she entered the room, peace ushered in around me. Her voice was like a whispering meadow, and it fell on my ears with comforting words that I liked to hear. Aunt Bobbie was someone we all leaned on throughout the years.

Mom pleaded with her sister to take me when I was born. She promised her there would be no strings attached, swearing to officially sign the permanent custody papers and never come back for me. As much as my aunt knew she would be my safe harbor, she just could not do it. Mom had dealt her those cards before, and Aunt Bobbie had finished with the losing hand.

Seven years earlier, Mom had placed my oldest sister, Wendy Sue, in Aunt Bobbie's arms. She was given no resources, and what was supposed to be babysitting for a few days, grew into almost a year without ever hearing from my mom. Wendy had fallen ill and came with no medical release or custody papers, which made the situation even more taxing. The pale-faced baby was suffering. After trying everything to help the crying child, Aunt Bobbie convinced her local doctor to stop by the house and check on her. Wendy had the flu, and the physician was compassionate enough to supply free medicine to help her recover. My dear sister quickly became Aunt Bobbie's world. She was the light of her life.

After a long absence, my mom returned, and without explanation said she wanted her baby back. With no care for Aunt Bobbie's feelings, Mom demanded her child. Given no choice, with tearstained cheeks and a broken heart, Aunt Bobbie said goodbye to the little girl who had occupied her time and filled her days with joy.

Mom's only responsibility was caring for Wendy. This was already more than she could handle. Jack and Vicky, my two siblings between Wendy and me, had both been living with Dad at the time. Once Aunt Bobbie declined her offer, Mom resigned herself to the situation, and with Wendy, brought me home to their single wide, well-kept trailer, which sat on a beautiful piece of landscaped property.

Walking outside, Wendy said she could see the towering Virginia Mountains from the lush land that bore apple trees and vines of wild strawberries. She described it as a place of serenity. When she wasn't inside romping around with me, Wendy spent her days climbing apple trees and picking luscious fruit that she could eat right off the tree or vine, lost in a world without cares.

Despite being told repeatedly to stay out of my crib, Wendy would get up during the night and crawl into my crib anyhow, to sleep beside me. She loved me and felt it was her life's mission to protect and adore me.

At about six months old, I was hospitalized for dehydration that led to pneumonia, which nearly took my life. Because of injections I had been given, the doctors had to shave the hair from my head. A family friend said I looked like a boy and nicknamed me Sam. Though Wendy passionately argued that my name wasn't Sam, it was a name that would stick with me through my college years and to this day among my family.

It is said that I was the child whose entrance was most unwanted. Instead of being terribly rejected, Mom's remorse over her first thoughts of giving me away stayed present with her, and I became the child who could do no wrong in her eyes. She did not say she loved me regularly, as parents normally would in a stable environment; her world was a fight for survival. As a little girl, I seldom got a window of understanding into her inner thoughts and painful struggles, except when she would put pen to paper and write one of us a song or a poem. It was a beautiful moment caught in the sands of time when she would articulate herself through words, and share them with us. A song I loved to hear her sing was written for me when I was just a little girl.

Born Among Hard Times

That's my little girl
Just born among hard times
And quite a little girl she is.

Within the course of every day
She laughs, she frowns, she cries
But like us all she has a dream
Her goals are set high.

She knows she'll never get to Hollywood
If all she does is play
So she wanders off to school each day
And works hard to make them A's

She parades around in dresses
And little high-heeled shoes
She primps before the mirror and says
Oh, this will never do

"She'd like to pick a guitar
And play piano keys
She smiles and says
Oh, Mom, I'll be a star

She crawls up in my lap
And says, oh look, you're getting gray
Mom, whatever's gonna happen
If you'd have to go away

What if there are no dollies
Or, I'm just too old to play
Mom, whatever's gonna happen
If I never learn to pray

That's my little girl
She was born among hard times
And quite a little girl she'll stay.

My Siblings

My siblings and I were kept together in our younger years. Soon after my birth, Mom moved back to Chicago, and in a very short time, she became an influential *madam*, controlling a large-scale prostitution ring. Running her business, she traveled extensively, leaving us with housekeepers. We missed Mom, but as small children, we found joy and mischief in each other's company.

Wendy was a dainty red-head with fair skin and a lightly freckled face. She had pretty hair, tiny hands and a tender heart. As the eldest, Wendy tried to be our defender, especially for me. Some of our housekeepers were, at times, neglectful and abusive, but Wendy always fought to protect us.

My brother, Jack, was very charming. He had a beautiful head of dark brown hair, a sea of sparkling blue eyes, and a smile that would cause anyone to grin. He was a modern day Tom Sawyer who was mischievous, imaginative, spontaneous and irrational. For the sake of conquering, he would lie, steal or cheat to hold the upper hand.

Vicky was my middle sister and would later become most like a friend, as we were the closest in age. She was tall, thin, and pretty, but in a tomboy sort of way. Her coffee shaded hair complemented her tan face that was sprinkled with a freckle here and there. With a strong personality that captured the  attention of those around her, Vicky was a natural in athletics and was always the best at whatever we did. Whether it was school, swimming, or softball, she had to be in first place. I loved my sister, and the world always seemed to be a better place when she was around. I felt safeguarded by her.

Crab Legs and Quarters

As a little girl, my favorite meal was Alaskan King Crab Legs. When fine dining was the order of business, there was always a much older rich man to cover the bill. We were told to order anything our hearts desired. If it was on the menu, I was going to nurture my love for king crab legs which for me, began at a very early age. Mom used to say she got as much joy from watching me dip my large chunks of crab meat into the hot, salty lemon butter as I got from gobbling every scrumptious bite. One Christmas season, I stood at the buffet and stuffed the side pockets of my velvet winter coat with as many King Crabs as I could fit into it, out of fear they would not be there on our next visit. I'm not sure what distressed Mom more, her thieving little girl, or the thought of my new Christmas coat saturated in crab juice. However, at that tender age, I was the apple of her eye. Instead of punishment, I was awarded a kiddy cocktail with peppermint ice cream to follow. This is the same mother, who years later, presented me with a stack of two-dollar bills and a roll of quarters to go shopping, *after* I'd been caught stealing a load of jewelry at the Walgreen's on Lake Street and was escorted home by the police. My sisters were furious with Mom's decision to baby me in this situation, but Mom said I wouldn't have had to take what wasn't mine if I would have had money of my own. In truth, throwing money at me was easier for her than actual parenting.

As the years passed, crab legs and quarters could not remedy all the frustrations, insecurities, and hurts I harbored in my heart. Never knowing where we would live, who Mom would fall in love with next, or whether we would spend our winters living in luxury or a tiny tent, presented many challenges for a young girl.

When I was three-years-old, we moved from Catawba Lane to a house in the country in St. Charles, located on a sprawling piece of land that included a swing hanging from an enormous, old oak tree. Although there was plenty of room downstairs, since Mom was never there, our housekeeper, Jane, made all of us sleep in the dusty attic. We slept upstairs, which was separated from the rest of the house, in makeshift rooms divided only by sheets for walls. Despite the dust and dirt, our laughter rippled through the house, and she would scream up the stairs for us to "tone it down!" Because I was a bed-wetter, Jane would force me to climb out the window onto the badly shingled roof, and hand wash my sheets. The intense heat from the sun would beat down on me as I trembled atop the fifteen-foot height with a bowl of water, a bar of soap, and soiled sheets. Once finished, she would line-dry my sheets and give me a good slap in the face saying, "Now maybe you'll stop wetting the bed, you little brat." At dinnertime, Jane would feed us liver and onions while she stood at the end of the kitchen table with a belt, threatening to hit one of us until we cried, if we did not clean our plates. I will never forget the day my mother walked in on this routine and rescued me. In all my days, I cannot remember another time that my mom was that kind.

After this rescue, Mom became dependent on one of her regular clients. Their relationship changed our lives as we were instantly plunged into a circle of higher society. Almost overnight, we became country club members, pranced around in high-end clothing, and were driven around in the finest cars because our new "Grandpa" owned a multi-million-dollar engineering company. Grandpa Clayton was several

27

decades older than Mom. She met him through her escort service that serviced mostly rich and powerful men with deep pockets. Clayton's goal was to save her as his most prized possession, but with Mom, that was not an option. Although he asked repeatedly, she would never marry him. He offered her the world on a silver platter, purchasing her two homes, allowing her to travel to far-away destinations, and buying her all the clothing, jewelry, cars, and perfume her heart desired.

Big Money and the Boogeyman

We had big money, endless clothes, beautiful cars, and luxury homes. During our first Christmas in the Monterey house, my sisters and I wore matching flowered dresses. The tables were lined with delicate china and gourmet food. I received a

Snoopy dog in my stocking, a box full of *Weeble Wobbles,* and every *Town and Country* building set that could be bought for them. We ate and played all day while many families came to visit with us.

While living here, my first encounter with the "boogeyman" occurred. I was four-years-old, I can truly say that I have vivid, haunting, memories of the *first* time hurt chose me! Mom was downstairs sitting in her favorite yellow chair, holding a scotch in one hand and a cigarette in the other, while she listened to Linda Ronstadt's latest release, "When Will I Be Loved." This is what I remember hearing when he came upstairs. He was a family friend, not a boyfriend of Mom's, just a guy she allowed to camp at our house after being released from prison or being thrown out of his house for the night.

He entered my room first and took turns messing with Vicky and me. His presence was eerie, and my skin crawled as he towered over us with evil desires. His hands were large and cold, and my heart pounded as I lay in fearful silence while he did his thing. One night when he finished robbing Vicky and me of peaceful sleep and restful dreams, he approached the door to Wendy's room. His vile presence immediately woke her. Wendy wasn't anything like us. She stood up on the bed, screamed to the top of her lungs, and demanded that he get out of her room. Wendy was small, but she feared no one. On future nights, when she knew he was around, she would stay awake and guard our doors before he had a chance to enter. She was the older sister, and she felt tremendous remorse over the times she knew she had not protected us. Looking back, none of us understand how this monster stayed a part of our lives throughout the years, showing up, lurking around, and planning to make another move. His actions seared horrible scars into my memory.

To an outsider, we were rich kids who had it all. For that stretch of time, we were pampered, but never protected. We were offered things, but not time. We knew luxury, but not real love. There were no bedtime rituals that included stories or prayer time. We were sent upstairs to fall asleep, while Mom either sold her body, drowned her sorrow in scotch, or sat in a chair in tears, probably wondering how she had arrived at this particular destination in life. She was powerful and beautiful. At this time, she could have left her work as a Madam, but she was too far down the rabbit hole, feeling trapped and taken, while staying with men two times her age. Regardless, she managed to make it work as long as possible.

Our Best Years

After living on Sea Biscuit Lane, Grandpa bought us a house in the beautiful town of Wheaton. I eagerly stared out the window as we drove up and down many long streets that eventually led to our new corner home. Standing on a hill, it looked like a fortress in my five-year-old mind. Getting out of the Lincoln, I smelled the fresh, cut grass from the perfectly manicured lawn. Flowers bloomed, and the bushes stood tall, as if at attention, to welcome us. Judy, the real estate lady, was waiting. She smiled, greeted us, and handed Mom the keys.

Walking into our new castle-home, we entered a big foyer with an enormous, extended room straight ahead. This would soon be a sitting space adjacent to the formal dining area, two rooms we were not allowed to enter. To the right, was a kitchen filled with large appliances and immaculate countertops. To the left, down a set of five carpeted stair-steps, was another separate, but attached apartment. This space held

an office, a bedroom, a full bathroom, a long and wide living room and a bar, similar to the ones where Mom and I sat in restaurants. From that room was a door hiding a mile-long descending staircase that led us to what I envisioned as a gigantic playroom, but they referred to it as a basement. From the foyer, we could go up a short flight of stairs that led to four bedrooms where sunlight poured in through large windows. At the end of the hall was the master suite that Mom shared with Grandpa. Inside, there was a large bathroom with massive walk-in closets and yet another place to bathe that looked more like a kiddie pool at the country club to me.

We were each given our own bedroom. When I walked into my room, I could smell the fresh pale pink paint. Before long, my space was adorned with sturdy, white wicker furniture and a row of china dolls that stretched across the top shelving. My bedframe sat high, and the mattress was like sleeping on a pillow of clouds. I would spend hours in that room, playing in a world of make-believe with my baby dolls that cried and sometimes peed on me. Each baby had a name, but "Jenny" was the one I called my best friend. Sometimes, I felt nervous in that house. When I did, I would run up the stairs and sit in my oversized rocking chair, swaying back and forth, cradling Jenny.

I loved that house, and I held an authentic adoration for Grandpa too. He was a tall man who wore expensive suits and a hat, and he smelled like the sweet cherry tobacco that he kept in his old pipe. However, for some reason, I still dreamed of someday having parents more like Nancy Balter's, my best friend from across the street. Nancy's parents looked like they were both the same age. Her family was Jewish, so during the holiday, they would allow me to come over each day to see what she received for Hanukah. They were good people who seemed to really care for one another. I also noticed that they had different household rules, such as when to come in at night and regularly scheduled bedtimes.

Sometimes Mom and Grandpa entertained people. I was taught to speak clearly and with confidence to whomever I was presented. Mom used to tell me  that her friends loved to hear me talk and tell colorful stories of the events from my playful days. She said my entertainment was often so good that she and Grandpa jokingly considered charging a fee for the privilege of attending the "show." I seriously thought I was a 1970's Shirley Temple, headed for stardom. I ate up the affection and attention I received, even if I was only amusing a crowd of adults who had consumed far too many mixed drinks.

Though this time period brought my siblings and me great joy, Mom still felt trapped and stuck. Those were my best years, even though I don't think Mom considered us much when making decisions. She and Grandpa were continually fighting because she did not like being tied down, so she packed us up and walked away. She was frustrated with his "demands" for her to be a stay-at-home mother, so she ran away in search of fulfillment.

Leaving Clayton

The next two years were filled with ridiculously absurd instability. We spent more time in Illinois, moving from place to place than we did staying in any one place, or so it seemed. We would go to school in tears, and we were introduced to bullying. During this time, I accidentally set a house on fire, while playing with matches on the couch. We spent hours on end at bars, playing video games while Mom worked as a bartender.

At the end of first grade, the phone rang. Though they were not together, Mom and Dad still talked often, but only as friends. Dad called Mom with stories about a former "john," who he felt loved her, and she couldn't get us to Florida fast enough. Living in the "Sunshine State" introduced me to several things I'd never seen before. We lived at the Four Seasons Apartment  Complex on Arlington Express Way. Mom worked at Red Lobster, which was within walking distance to our apartment. Moving there was different and strange. Mom had moved us out of our mini-mansion on a hill to our third dingy apartment since leaving our beautiful house, and we soon filled it with a complete set of build-it-yourself, pressed-wood furniture. Until now, I had never seen a roach. They traveled in colonies, both inside and outside of our new home. I saw a lot of salamanders and lizards and complained how terribly hot it was all the time.

It was good to see Dad on occasion, but his lifestyle and friends were frightening. I vividly recall the day Wendy picked up the phone and heard, "The *outlaws* are coming! The *outlaws* are coming!" I could hear the fear in her voice from across the room. Our step-mother, Miriam, was on the other end of the phone. She was talking to Wendy in a loud voice, and it was clear to me that she was scared. Dad was coming home with the *outlaws*.

A drug deal was going down, and Miriam knew it would end badly. She did not want any of the kids around. Vicky and Jack were living with her and Dad at the time, and Miriam brought them all to stay with Wendy and me until the dust cleared. Dad had grown from pimp to drug dealer who lived without fear of consequences.

It did not take long for Mom's latest love interest, Ricky, to break her heart. After this heartbreak, Mom mixed a cocktail of orange juice and rubbing alcohol in an attempt to end her life. I cried myself to sleep, wondering if she would live to see my next birthday. But, live she did. After spending a few days in the hospital, Mom decided it was time to go home. So, we packed up our pressed wood furniture and headed back north. It was 1979, and the catastrophic events ahead would soon bring great change to our lives.

Mom took us back to what she knew. We rented an apartment on the corner of Lake Street and Greenbrook Boulevard, living across the street from a bar called the Thirsty Camel, where Mom had an established client base. During this time, she reconnected with Grandpa Clayton. For the next seven months, they would reestablish their relationship and at the end of second grade, he took us home to our mini-mansion on the hill. I can't tell you how relieved I was to return to that house. Though it held some unwanted memories, Florida was worse because it had brought many terrifying experiences for me, and I was glad to leave that state.

During this season of our lives, we were again blessed with the material things we had previously grown accustomed to having. However, our lives were still surrounded with instability because Mom was turning tricks behind Grandpa's back. She was a severe alcoholic, and her mental health was fragile. Instead of seeking real help from a counselor or a church, she drowned her sorrows in scotch.

Dad, along with twenty-five of his *associates*, was arrested on October 25 of 1979, for running a multi-million-dollar drug ring. Dad was considered the King Pin. Someone had tipped him off that the authorities were coming. He called Miriam to warn her. The next day, the police and news crews showed up at the house at 6 AM to arrest him. He wasn't there, but later he turned himself in to the police. There was no way around it. They had been tapping his phone for over sixty days. Later, Dad and Harrison, one of his closest cohorts, would be sentenced to prison for fifteen years. Even though I wasn't close to my father, I loved him dearly, and this day would change my life. Here we were, living in Wheaton, Mom, a prisoner to alcohol, and Dad was a prisoner to the state of Florida.

During this same time, Grandpa was diagnosed with liver cancer. His sickness came fast and furiously. Grandpa loved my Mom more than life itself, but during his illness, a family member came to visit and told him that he needed to change his will. Though Mom was fulfilling her duties to nurture him during his health crisis, he found out that she was still meeting with many of her regulars. Even with the promise of millions that would soon be all hers, she could not be faithful. This broke Grandpa's heart. He did not kick us out, and he never uttered a word to Mom. He loved her until his dying day, but he changed her expected financial future.

I was in Mrs. Quarter's third grade class the day the call came. Grandpa had passed away, and in that moment, my life would forever change. I would never again know of wealth. I would never eat another dripping ice cream cone from the country club, or receive another box of Fannie May candies on Sunday afternoons. There would be no more high-end shopping sprees or thousand-dollar Christmases. The mention of a housekeeper, a cook, or stretched-out vehicles with leather interior would never again be in my world. Yes, those days were not always easy. Yes, we still bore pain, but those were my best years. The memories from having had a taste of it all would never leave me.

Grandpa did not leave Mom his millions. Indeed, *if* she had been smart, we could have been set for life. She had enough money to not only survive, but to invest and build a respectable life for herself. However, none of that was possible with Mom. She squandered every resource. She had to find a way to be used, abused, trafficked, and hurt. She could not make the most of real opportunities, so life got worse.

From fourth through sixth grade, we were basically homeless, but Mom had an uncanny ability to get people to allow us into their home. She carried herself in a way that drew men from all walks of life. She would paint her face with minimal makeup and finish it off with a dark reddish or muted burnt orange lipstick. When she was dressed to the nines, her mood would lift. Though her choice to engage in selling her body left her broken and insecure, the need to be wanted was her greatest addiction. She sold her self-worth in exchange for shelter and provision. She had dreams of love, but she trusted no one, so in reality, love truly was not an option.

I vividly remember Mom recklessly speeding down the interstate with a drink in one hand and a cigarette in the other.

She would travel with us for days, looking for a new place to land. We would ask, "Are we there yet?"

Mom's reply was, "No, because I don't have a clue where we are going!" Every once in a while, she would stop for gas and put a quarter in the phone booth, making a call to someone who could possibly help us. I would muster up the courage to ask about the school we just left, and she would say, "You don't go there anymore. We will find you a new school."

One of the most exciting stops for us kids was McDonald's. It wasn't the food that lured us; it was the monopoly money. We would collect stamps across the states, and we truly believed that we would be winners one day! Other than a lot of large fries and milkshakes, we never did win much, but the game kept our minds off our present situation of being homeless with a lady who lived life on the edge.

Sometimes, Mom left us with a friend, a stranger, or a relative. She lived without agenda or consequence and with no thought for what tomorrow held. She would pack us up and take us anywhere she deemed safe while she would "go and clear her head, sort things out, or make more money." These times of abandonment created grave insecurity for me.

Thankfully, I had learned how to work the crowd as a little girl growing up in Wheaton. In no time at all, I would be doing whatever the adults caring for me required to keep peace while making a new set of neighborhood friends to occupy my time. As bad as things were when Mom was around, I lived in anticipation of the day she would return. When we were apart, I would sob daily until she would once again return with open arms, empty promises, and freshly-penned songs. An old favorite she would sing to me and my sisters was about the home we all knew best. It was in the form of a highway.

Girls sit down and listen
As I help you understand
The wanderings of a woman
When she's looking for a man

I don't want to be alone
once you're grown and gone
So I need to find a man
who can love and understand
That there's more to life and happiness
Than a list of plain demands.

Tomorrow, we're leaving,
going back on that road.
For that long and lonely highway
is the only home I'll ever know.

Mom's Rage

Until our lives were spent on the run, we never saw Mom's anger. Because we lived in a state of constant hopelessness, Mom became abusive. I remember a time when Vicky accidentally put away a slightly spotted cup into the cabinet, and Mom went ballistic. After crashing it to the floor, she proceeded to make Vicky take every single dish out of the kitchen cabinets and forced her to wash, dry, and put them all back away.

On many occasions, we would wake up at 2 AM to the sound of dishes crashing on the floor. If we did not wake up and go downstairs, she came for us. Mom thought nothing of grabbing one or two of us by our hair and dragging us down the stairs. She threw pots and pans, and screamed because the house was not clean enough. We were all in tears, running around in our pajamas, trying to please her, and calm her down. Inevitably, by morning, she would present us with some form of apology, but we were still to blame.

On many Saturdays, she would empty all of our drawers and tell us we had one hour to put our clothes away correctly. Toys and anything else she could grab, were thrown into a heap in the middle of the floor. Whatever remained when the clock finished ticking, went to the dumpster. We never knew when these fits would come, but her shouting remained a constant in our lives.

I only suffered at the hand of Mom's fist once. I was an athlete in high school when this occurred, yet I was sure Mom was still stronger than me. She was small but played dirty, so I surrendered and left the room with a broken heart. I had seen her fight with Wendy too many times, and I knew I could not win, not that I even wanted to *win*. One time she had beat Wendy's head into the ground and held a flowerpot over her head, threatening to drop it on her head. Mom had threatened to kill her more times than I can count. The catalyst for many family feuds reaching an out-of-control level, was when one of us strongly disagreed with Mom or talked back to her in any form or fashion. She would slap us across the face at the first sign of disrespect; it simply was not tolerated. I loved, hated, and feared her all at the same time.

To be honest, waking up to Mom in a fit of rage was admittedly less scary than some of the other things I had slowly scooted down the stairs to witness. Afraid and unsure of emerging events, I would flip a switch and witness sights far too graphic for a book penned by me. Instead of shame on Mom's part, she would rattle off a string of cuss words and tell me to get back upstairs. I would run for my life, lock my bedroom door, and hide under the covers waiting for morning to come.

In the Kitchen

After the time period of housekeepers ended, when I was finishing third grade, I remember more days of waking up without my mom at home, begging her for a bowl of cereal if she was home, and sometimes fighting my siblings for the last drop of milk. Despite the pain, there were good days with Mom. My fondest memories were formed in the kitchen. It was a place where she smiled. I recall a day when she was sober and happy. She made us a stuffed spinach omelet, centered among perfectly cut cantaloupe, bananas, and kiwi, with a side of nine-grain toast, kissed with a sloppy dab of butter, and a large glass of freshly squeezed orange juice.

I remember Mom cooking more when we were older, and when she did, it was all from scratch. I would sit for hours and watch her make gourmet holiday candies, chocolate cream pies, coconut cakes, and tiramisu. Most of my friends feared my mom because she drank too much and had a violent temper, but everyone liked to come around when the table was set. Meals were offered with glass plates, linen napkins, and food fit for a king. We were the only people I knew who served shrimp dijon as an appetizer. When Mom prepared a spread, we never ate instant potatoes or boxed macaroni. My father was a five-star chef, and he had taught Mom how to cook. I believe my mother even surpassed my dad in her culinary abilities because she enjoyed cooking so much.

Raising Ourselves

Mom was running the Chili Pub and turning tricks on the side when she met Klaus. I was eleven at the time, and we were living in a rented town house on Kit Carson Drive, attending our third school for that year. Vicky turned thirteen. Jack was fifteen, but due to his delinquent behavior, he was living in a boy's home. Wendy gave birth to her first son at the age of seventeen.

Our landlord had just purchased a red, shiny, truck. He washed it religiously and had asked us not to throw our ball anywhere near the parking lot. One day, I got this creative inkling to not only spray-paint the water meters, but to also spray-paint the truck. Being eleven, I clearly knew better, but I was bored, and with boredom often came mischief. The mixture of that little act of terrorism, coupled with Wendy's boyfriend driving his vehicle through the neighbor's living room, caused us to be evicted. So yet again, we were moving, but this time we did not go far. Because of embarrassment, it was the one time I actually longed to attend another school with a fresh set of challenges, even if it did include living under the radar until I found safety among new friends.

The worst part of this move was living in Carpentersville and attending school with the rich kids from Barrington. This caused us shame and bullying. I knew enough about *having it all*, but I could not imagine being unkind, like so many of the wealthy kids were. I hated the words spoken from the teacher, "Class, today we have a new student." It was the most painful experience. That ten-second introduction always felt like an eternity. Luckily for me, with a quick glance around the classroom, I once again managed to choose the kid I hoped to win over as my friend. This did not always work out as perfectly as I hoped, but it did so more often than not.

We must accept finite disappointment,
but never lose infinite hope.
Martin Luther King Jr

Homeless and Hungry

A few days after Mom and Klaus split, because they had been fighting, she met two men at the bar. These were good looking, fast-talking guys who promised us a home in Tampa, Florida. They colorfully portrayed all that it would entail, even down to the speaker systems that would run throughout our bedrooms. The anticipation was all very exhilarating. Mom was persuaded to sell all of our finest furniture and move, while we looked forward to sunnier days in a warmer climate. What we did not sell, Mom loaded up and stored in the neighbor's garage. We were packed and ready to go when the guys said they were going to run to the gas station in Mom's Datsun and be right back to get us. A ten-minute drive turned into ten hours, and we soon realized that we had been robbed.

Within days, "Uncle Scott" showed up. He was a creepy guy, who had been in and out of our lives for years. Although none of us trusted him, we had no other option at the time. As a family, we had nothing more than each other, and now there was a new *boogeyman* to fear in the midnight hours.

My brother Jack was in a lot of trouble with the law, and he was due to appear in court in just a few days. His situation did not look good. Instead of finding a home nearby, we fled the state, taking Jack with us.

We spent a couple of weeks in Oklahoma, at Uncle Scott's parents' house. They offered us beds, food, and entertainment, while Mom and Scott figured out what to do next.

I'm not sure why, but from Oklahoma we headed to Texas. We spent the week of Thanksgiving, in Arlington, living in a hotel. Our entertainment was swimming in the pools during the day; our meals were downtown, with the homeless people. Getting food meant standing in long lines, and Mom would tell us to stay away from the video cameras, unless we wanted to be on television. We could only afford one room, so Uncle Scott took turns sleeping with Jack or Vicky each night in the van. This was not a fun experience for my older siblings. Looking back, I'm glad I was never chosen. After a week of having our own room, Vicky came down with a terrible toothache. Because we couldn't afford a doctor, she was continually given Jack Daniels to drink. Inevitably, she got drunk for the first time, at age thirteen. Mom took one look at her and said, "Get out of my face. You make me too sick to even look at you." Mom soon found some clients to hook up with, buying us another week in the hotel, before we had to move to yet another city.

Our next stop was Brownsville, Texas. Somehow, we had found a house we thought we could rent. We had no deposit, but we promised the owners it would be forthcoming within a few weeks. On our first night in the house, supper was a shared can of watered-down, chicken-noodle soup. Remembering being scared and hungry, Vicky said it was the only time in her life that she felt sure she would starve to death. That night, Mom sang us songs and tried to help us feel less afraid.

The next morning, Uncle Scott got up and drove to a nearby Naval Base. Somehow, he managed to come home with two buckets of fried chicken and endless bags of groceries. We unpacked the bags and put away boxes of cereal, canned goods, and all sorts of meat and dairy products. It was like manna from heaven. However, our excitement was short-lived.

The next morning, we awoke to a knock at the door. It was the landlord and his wife. We did not know the reason why, but they apologized to us and said that our arrangement with them just was not going to work. They gave us one-hundred dollars and asked that we please leave by morning. We were devastated. With no place else to go, Scott returned to his parents, who gave us a green Chevy van and a tent that was supposed to be our home. From there, we headed to the KOA Campground in Quinlan, Texas.

We pitched our tent and parked the van. The first night, rain pounded our tiny tent, so we grabbed our heavy blankets and managed to sleep in the clunky van. In the back, Vicky, Scott,  and Jack, slept side by side. I slumbered on the middle bench, and Mom dozed on and off, sitting up in the front seat. It was miserable and cold, but we were survivors. After that, we only used the tent during the day, and that is the way we lived for the next several months.

Mom enrolled Vicky and me in Quinlan Middle School. I was in sixth grade, and Vicky was in eighth grade. Some of my recollections of that time include sleeping in the van, waiting in line for a shower in the campground bathroom, catching the school bus from the KOA entrance, and being constantly questioned by classmates as to why I lived on a campground. Those were cutting, hurtful questions that were too painful to answer. I brushed them off, believing they just would not understand. It was all about survival, and part of surviving included dismissing what others thought of us. Some of the highlights of living in that setting included gathering the children to sing Christmas carols to neighboring campers. I enjoyed meeting normal families who invited me to sit outside with them, and taught me how to play card games. Oftentimes, these friendly neighbors questioned me about where my family called home, and asked how long we planned to be camping, while feeding me a warm bowl of soup or campfire potatoes.

I knew that Christmas would be a difficult morning, and I expected no presents under the tree. Nonetheless, Mom was resourceful and somehow managed to surprise us. I was shocked to receive a hand-held Pac-man game. Vicky was given a sixteen-sided Rubik's cube and a Missing Link. Jack was given some other sort of game, but I can't recall what it was.

As a twelve-year-old girl, I frequently would lie awake, staring aimlessly into the twinkling lights that shone so brightly from our humble Christmas tree in the tiny tent.

I vividly remember a life-changing moment when my mother reached over to me, brushed her hand across my face, and kindly asked, *"Why are you still awake? What are you thinking about?"*

I replied, *"Mom, I'm thinking about hope, and how I hope that one day my life will shine as bright as the bulbs on our tree."*

Mom looked me in the eyes and gently patted my back saying, *"Your life already shines baby girl, and I know it always will. You are my little girl. You were born among hard times, but quite a little girl you'll stay."* That was one of those special moments I have held onto in times of despair. Her words of comfort on that particular night, have been forever etched into my mind. My mom memorialized our time in the KOA Campground with the following words.

On a Tent Floor

On a grey and misty morning,
in a campsite off somewhere,
lies a few unspoken memories
of a time that we once shared.

December wind oh how it whistled.
December rain, oh how it fell.
On a tent floor how the mud ran
and there we sat in a wore out Chevy van.

Christmas loomed a gloomy one.
The skies were dark and grey,
On a table sat a Christmas tree
Oh 4 feet high I'd say.

The LIGHTS were strung in sequence
for all the world to see.
The packages were minimal
but all that we could need.

December wind, oh how it whistled,
December rain, oh how it fell,
On a tent floor how the mud ran
and there we sat in a wore out Chevy van.

While we were at the KOA, Mom found a job and was finally able to move us into a trailer park. We changed schools, and during this time, Vicky told an adult that Scott had been molesting her. This man told Mom, and she was furious with Vicky and called her a liar. Though Mom knew the truth, she could not admit that her choices were causing us harm, so she chose to deny it. Meanwhile, Vicky had made a new friend, Shannon, and began spending all of her time at Shannon's house, while I was being regularly left alone. Because of the allegations Vicky made against Scott, he left, and Mom became restless. Sensing our need for help, Shannon's dad told Vicky if she ever felt the need, she was welcome to move in with them. Vicky liked the idea and introduced Mom to Shannon's parents. Within a few minutes, Mom was releasing Vicky into their care and saying, "I'm going to head to Dallas. Do you mind keeping Sam too?" They were happy with the arrangement, and in no time at all, my sister and I were packed and living in a trailer in the country, with a family that included six kids. During this same time, Jack kept getting into a lot of trouble with the law and was sent to a boys' home for discipline.

Country Life

Our home was surrounded by large trees and long winding, gravel roads. Even though this family had six children, they often took in strays, like me and my sister. They did not claim a Christian connection by any stretch of the imagination, but their home provided a bed and three square meals a day. They did not have a lot of money, but we weren't hungry, mostly eating what we caught and killed. Squirrel, fish, and rabbits were served at dinnertime, and we learned to like it. On a sour note, we had to eat liver and onions once a week, and we were NOT allowed to leave the table until our plates were cleared. I managed by swallowing a spoonful of ketchup with every bite.

There were no rules with this family. If we wanted to drink a beer, smoke a joint, be intimately involved with someone else, or go skinny dipping, it was allowed. Everything was okay, as long as they knew where we were. It was during this time, I learned to fight, cuss, and fend for myself. This family taught us street smarts. We learned that if the Department of Family Services came for a visit, run into the woods, and flee from the law.

I also learned several positive habits while living with this rescue family. I learned the discipline of becoming an early riser. Stepping outside in the early morning, I literally discovered the meaning of "before the cock's crew." Breathing in the clean air, I learned responsibility, since it was my job to feed the chickens and goats. Unwillingly, I even learned how to behead a chicken, dip it in the scalding bin of hot water, and pull off the feathers as part of the preparation process to have fried chicken for dinner.

Here in this country place, I could play outside for hours and experience the outdoors as a kid. Thoughts of my mom were always close to my heart, but I was happy in this quasi-farming atmosphere. I was happy even when we did not have running water and had to pile into the back of Bob's pick-up truck with 60 milk jugs and head to town every day for water, or when we had to stay a few extra minutes in the lake for our weekly bath.

When it was decided that it was time to build a new house, I learned how to hammer a nail and help with the construction. It was a five room house. The great room contained a large picnic table for our meals. Even with all of the craziness, the huge picnic table brought routine and normalcy, as we gathered around it to eat. The house had no air-conditioning, and a potbellied stove was our heating system. The rooms were framed, but the walls were covered with sheets for separation and privacy.

We lived with this family for one year before Mom wrote us a letter to say she was coming to get us. She had contacted Aunt Bobbie for help, and Aunt Bobbie came to the rescue. She packed up everything she owned in Arizona and moved to Dallas to help Mom set up an apartment that would be our new home. Mom pulled up in the middle of the night, laid on the horn, woke up the household, and told Vicky and me it was time to go. We headed to Dallas.

Two Sisters Work Together

Both Mom and Aunt Bobbie secured jobs at the nearby country club. I was allowed to visit them, go for a swim, and get free food whenever I wanted. Aunt Bobbie was promoted to the tennis court bar, and Mom became jealous. It was during this time that I attended my first dance. Aunt Bobbie

took me shopping and bought me a beautiful shirt and skirt. She fixed my make-up and hair, loaned me her jewelry, and sent me on my way. That night was a favorite and lasting memory in my young life.

Throughout this period, the two sisters were blessed to meet many celebrities. Mom dated Greg, and Aunt Bobbie dated his brother, David. Initially they were splitting expenses, but before long, they began arguing, so Aunt Bobbie and David moved to California.

Once Aunt Bobbie left, Mom had to work even more in order to support us. While she worked, I ran the streets with a rough gang of kids. We listened to rock and roll, partied, went to concerts, attended professional wrestling matches, played football, and stole from stores. It was this Christmas when I was arrested for stealing over $500 worth of jewelry and clothes. Mom made me stay at the jail for hours in hopes that the experience would scare me. She was right. I was frightened beyond comprehension.

A few weeks after the arrest, I was raped by a neighbor the day of my thirteenth birthday party. The decision was made to send me back to the country to live with the family on the farm. I was hurt beyond repair, and Mom had no ability to help me. This decision seemed like a good solution to her.

Have you ever been hurt and the place tries to heal a bit,
and you just pull the scar off of it over and over again?
Rosa Parks

Back to the Country

As much as I wanted to return to this family, it was nothing like the first time I lived with them. Dad had gotten out of prison, and Vicky had gone to live with him in Florida. So this time, I was alone. I came back to them with a great level of pain in my life, and their lives also seemed to have changed in many ways. There were a lot of whispered secrets, shady activity with strange visitors coming and going, family abuse, and much more.

Life being so taxing, it was here I learned to fight, and I still have the scars to prove it. If you squabbled with a sibling, or any other kid in the house, you were told to take it outside where the fight resumed to near death. I let that *tough girl* attitude bleed over to the schoolhouse. Previously, I had never been a bully or much of a fighter, but after weeks of an older girl picking on me every day, I finally lost control. She had pushed me one too many times. Against what should have been my better judgment, I shoved her forcefully enough into the school's trophy case to shatter the glass and propel her into a hospital bed. Although I suffered an in-school suspension, I was applauded for finally standing up for myself. As a result, I was never picked on again by anyone, on the bus, or in that school. I had made a name for myself.

There was tension in the home, and I was becoming increasingly fearful that something was happening around me. Even though I did not really know or understand what it was, I felt an urgency to leave. But, it wasn't going to happen just yet.

The Texas Cowboy

Living in chaos, I found a glimmer of normalcy and hope in the form of budding love. Tyler was his name, and he was my first love. I met him in that old country school, and he dominated every moment of my thoughts. He was a junior when I was a freshman. Medium build with shoulder length sandy blonde hair, he was a Dallas Cowboy, loving dude, dressed in Wrangler jeans and well-worn boots. The first time he gazed at me from across the classroom, I turned around to see if he was for certain looking at me. Our relationship started with a simple note, the first of many more to letters and poems to follow.

I darted out of class, headed for my locker, and he followed close behind. Infatuation with him was instant. This *dude* loved to talk and listen. Tyler cared about me, was interested in my life, and found my stories fascinating, besides being kind and treating me with respect. With all this attention, including writing me poetry, our friendship soon grew into teenage love.

Meanwhile, the situation at the home I was in had taken a turn for the worse, and I knew I needed to move away. The man of the house tried to molest me, but I pushed him away and told him "No." When Mom called to check on me, I told her I needed to relocate and why. In no time, she contacted my sister Wendy and made arrangements for me to move to Chicago and live with her. When the time came for me to leave Texas, my boyfriend and I both shed our share of tears. I would miss him. I would even miss the people I was living with, but I no longer felt safe. I packed my bags and told my country family goodbye.

Tyler drove me to Dallas. We stayed overnight with his mom before he drove me to the airport to catch my flight. His mother was blonde-headed and petite with soft skin that showed no sign of wrinkles. Her hands were gentle and smelled of fresh perfume. I asked her how she got her hands so soft, and she told me that she put lotion on them quite frequently. She spoke words I'd never heard before. She talked of God and His will, peace, love, joy. It did not transform my life that day, but a seed had been planted that would grow. We stayed up late than night talking and laughing. I enjoyed hearing stories about Tyler as a little boy.

The sun rose the next morning and we enjoyed a nice breakfast, took a lot of photos, and said a long goodbye in the Dallas airport before I boarded the plane and flew to the north side of Chicago. I cried the entire flight but knew this chapter of my life needed to come to a close.

City Streets

Wendy had become a teenage mom at the age of seventeen. She did not plan it that way, but it was inevitable. She had been playing house since a young age and was not unaware of the consequences that came with certain choices. To her, life was meant to be lived without thoughts of tomorrow or regrets of yesterday. She had met a bad boy named Dan, and their crazy dangerous love story soon led to the birth of my precious nephew, Jason. Wendy went to live at a home for pregnant teens but was determined to keep her little boy. He was born when Wendy was still a baby herself. Despite the circumstances, he was a welcomed infant, even by our mom. Though great dysfunction surrounded his birth, both his parents loved him dearly. He brought joy and change, the biggest change being that my sister grew up immediately.

At the time of my move to the city, Jason was four-years-old, and he was Wendy's whole world. Wendy was living as a single mom since Dan was currently serving time in jail. Together, mom and son helped me unpack my bag, welcoming me into their tidy apartment. Jason was a sandy-haired, perfectly happy and exceptionally clever young child. Wendy worked at the gas station down the road. While she worked, I would babysit this gloriously free little *fella*. We would rock back and forth on the couch, singing rhymes and songs and giggling to our hearts content. When I was with this little boy, who was full of only innocent fun, I hoped that Wendy could always keep him as happy as he was right at that moment. Don't get me wrong. They were barely getting by, but he was loved, nurtured, fed, and protected. That was all he needed at the time.

Wendy was not only good to me, but also felt it was her job to keep me safe. She did, still I was curious and a little bored, so I took walks to the park and sat on the benches a while before heading to the local dime store for an orange crush and a handful of candy. It did not take long for a group of young men to notice me. My heart still yearned for my Texas boyfriend, so my loyalty to that far-away love kept me safe from disastrous decisions. Just the same, I was running the streets of Chicago, learning about gangs such as the *Folks* and the *People*. The future for me could have quickly turned ruinous. I had befriended a group of teens who seemed to genuinely like me and accepted me for who I was, but they were friends with a rough world. Thank God, I was never sucked into their lifestyle, although it could have easily transpired.

The day we witnessed a gang fight right outside of Wendy's front window became the day my sister felt I needed a change. Wendy made a phone call. Within a week, I was headed to the suburbs to live with my mom and Klaus in Roselle. They were back together. Klaus was a nice looking, middle-aged man with a small frame, reddish blonde hair, and a set of bright blue eyes. He had lived in the states since the age of eighteen and still held the same job he had come to receive. He was still married to an Asian wife he had met as a young man serving in the German military. He had not laid eyes on her in years, but out of obligation to her, she received forty percent of his weekly paycheck. Klaus traveled out-of-state as an engineer and stayed in bars when he was home. He was a high-functioning alcoholic, but I didn't care because I was always safe in his presence. Later in life, Mom ended up marrying Klaus when I was in college.

Because my Mom lacked the ability to discipline me, she quickly allowed my Texas boyfriend to hop on a train and move in with us in our tiny, two-bedroom apartment. Mom worked around the clock, bartending and doing whatever else it was she did, so my boyfriend and I were left to our own devices. Tyler wanted to do his part, so he quickly found work. It was strange saying goodbye to him each morning as he walked me to the bus stop. I was a sophomore, and none of my friends could believe I had a real live cowboy living in my home. As heartbreaking as it was for both of us, a few months into this new arrangement, Mom put him on a one-way train back to Texas. Our season together ended.

Cross-Country and Track

I had attended twenty-three schools by the tenth grade, and to say that was easy would be a lie. The constant changes forced me to be outgoing, and my boldness came through determination to be accepted. I soon found acceptance in a new attraction, sports.

Desiring to fill my emptiness, I made popularity my life during high school. In my sophomore year, I joined the cross-country and track teams. Finally, I began to find my place. I wasn't a great runner at first. In fact, I was a little overweight and the slowest one on the team. Klaus and Mom only came to one of my meets, and on that day, I finished in last place out of approximately 256 girls from across the state. Klaus later told me to find a new, more suitable passion, but I was determined. Losing did nothing more than give me a greater desire to figure out what it would take to get faster. I spent the next few months in pursuit of excellence. Exercise and running became my god. By the start of eleventh grade, I was fifth on our Varsity Cross-Country team and was voted team co-captain alongside my friend, Vonnie. I was running beside the best of them. My teammates gave me the love and affection for which I was longing, and my coach pushed me to excellence. We ran six days a week and worked races on most Sundays. Some of my friends were Christians and attended church regularly. That sounded boring to me and I would talk them into skipping services so we could have fun at the Sunday races. Our coach would have us pass out water as the athletes

ran past us. In return, we were rewarded with free fruit and a new t-shirt. I loved the thrill of these events.

I did not care much for classwork, but I did what was necessary. I believe that because I had lived in so many places and discovered so many different environments along the way, I'd developed a keen ability of bringing people together, while inspiring others to achieve goals. My friends saw something in me, so I sought to be a light in their lives. After this experience of achievement in sports and new-found popularity, I told myself that no matter what happened with Mom, I was digging in my heels and would graduate from Lake Park High School. I did move an additional three times during the process, but I did not change schools again.

Admittedly, in high school, I dabbled a few times with death through the experimentation of smoking pot and drinking alcohol, but for the most part, I stayed clean. I wanted my life to count for something. I didn't know what that meant at the time, but God was sparing me for a higher calling. Running track and being a leader were important parts of my life. Even though I had no knowledge of Jesus or the fact that He loved me, I constantly found myself trying to somehow save people.

Janice was a round-faced, blonde-haired tennis player whose blue eyes sat perfectly in her face. Her eyes were always searching for something inside of mine. She was talented both in sports and school, and I admired that about her. I'd never been much of a scholar, and she was at the top of the class. Though gifted, pretty, and quite clever in my eyes, she could not see herself as I did. Because of her low self-esteem, she seldom looked up or smiled. I noticed in the lunchroom, she ate alone. Seeing her day after day with no one to share her lunchtime was heartbreaking, and I felt it was my job to change it. Conversely, I had everything going for me. I had friends, and I had success on the track team, but something gravitated me toward her, pulling me closer with each passing day. I could not shake it. I wanted to know and understand her. I was compelled to interrupt her world.

One day I reached out to Janice. She was shocked and taken back by my candidness. I introduced myself and let her know that we would now be friends. She accepted my gesture, but I could instantly see that if our friendship developed, it was going to be on her terms. I was okay with that. I'd been hurt enough to see and realize when someone was hurting. While Janice may have felt invisible in a crowded room, she was no longer invisible to me. Besides her neighbor, who had taken his own life a few years earlier, I became her first real friend. Though I was busy being popular among my group of track and cross-country teammates, I was constantly feeling pulled toward her. She enjoyed my attention, and I quickly became the most important person in her life. She would stop me in the hallway to read one of her poems. They were dark, and many spoke of suicide. Then she wrote a poem for me. I had no direction or thoughts of how I could do it, but I knew I was somehow destined to help her. I knew it from the day I sat on the cold corner floor of the hallway, listening to her talk, my mind swirling with questions and possible answers about this deep, thought-provoking girl, who in all my travels, was unlike anyone I'd ever met.

My Visit to the Happy People's Church

At the age of seventeen, the built-up walls of my childhood finally began to crumble. I was working in Roselle, Illinois, at McDonalds, which stood on the corner of Irving Park and Maple Streets, just across from the town's busy train station. I worked there a few days after school and every Sunday night.

I was standing in my usual place behind the counter, wearing a cheerful smile. Although I did not quite know it at the time, a part of my heart groaned with agony and pain.

It was that time again. A river of sheer joy flowed into our restaurant as we rushed to make the decaffeinated coffee and cheeseburgers. The "happy people" were here again! Their faces beamed with light, and I listened with intensity to every word they spoke. Who *were* they? What made them so *different* from the regular "churchgoers" we served? While witnessing to me, a man they referred to as Bro. Abernathy, urged me to come visit. He told me that their church was unlike any other. I asked him in what way. He said it was similar to a football game, only they were cheering for God, and I could even talk and ask questions if I so desired. That seemed rather odd, but it also peaked my interest.

On that particular night, they introduced me to their drummer. He was a broad-shouldered young man with dark hair and nice eyes. With a friendly smile complimenting his blue suit, he ordered a chocolate milkshake. I wondered why such a good-looking guy spent so much time with church-going people. His name was Jason, and before leaving that night, he and his close friend invited me to church. Knowing I had to work Sundays, I refused their offer, but I was suddenly even more curious. For the next few days, I thought a lot about those two boys. In my mind, I questioned, why did they love God? I pondered whether their faith was real and kept wondering why those boys loved going to the church-house. It puzzled me.

On the fourth night of their week-long revival, the milkshake drinker, Jason, drove up at the drive-through window, and I happened to take his order. He asked me if I wanted to go on a date with him but stipulated that I would have to first attend Sunday School. Without any hesitation, I accepted his offer.

 That Sunday morning, I awoke at 7:30, leaving myself two hours to prepare for my visit to the "happy people's church." I wore a skin-tight, peach mini-dress with a spiked wrap-around belt and black leather boots. An array of plastic bracelets dangled from each of my wrists, and I wore my favorite pair of earrings. This was one of my special-occasion outfits.

Walking in, I was welcomed with foreign expressions such as "Praise the Lord!" and "We're so glad you came!" I felt as if I were their only guest.

I cannot remember what was taught in Sunday School, but they invited me to attend the six o'clock service as well. I was amazed at the hours these people spent in church. Feeling as if the entertainment would do me some good, I accepted the offer.

I sat in awe the entire service. I never prayed or dared to act like one of those fruitcakes, but I watched everything. By the middle of the service, people were spread all over the sanctuary. Some were crying, others were laughing, and apparently two were filled with what they called the Holy Ghost. Although I stood confused and maybe even somewhat afraid, I asked myself, "Could this be what I needed? What my new friend, Janice, needed?"

That night I only slept one hour. I tore down every Cyndi Lauper, Prince, and Michael Jackson rock poster off my ceiling and walls. Without even a small amount of real understanding, I made the unconscious decision that this church was for me. I had found a refuge of happiness. While I loved the camaraderie and thrill of what sports had brought me, this place was doing something to my heart. I suddenly felt less angry and afraid, and I wanted to know more about their God and why He made them all so *happy*.

A week later, they took me to a youth rally in Des Plaines, Illinois. I don't remember what the evangelist preached, but I sat in awe the entire service. Their music sounded like a symphony of joy. With each song, they would stand and raise their hands in adoration to the Lord. During the altar call, some lady asked me if I wanted to go up front and pray. Well, to be truthful, I said that I had a bit of a headache, but with the next breath, I found myself holding her hand. With little hesitation, I allowed the lady to take me up to the front for prayer. I had no clue what was going to come next! Suddenly, my body was shaking, and I was ready to release years of bondage from my soul.

Conviction of sin brought me to my knees, and I crumbled and wept. I did not even clearly understand repentance, but I was suddenly telling God that I would give Him every part of me. People surrounded me from all directions. They held me up as showers of tears flowed from my face. I did not care who was around me, or what was happening. Tingling sensations rushed through my arms, and my hands shook uncontrollably.

Although I had witnessed others receiving the Holy Ghost, I'd not yet heard about speaking in tongues. After about an hour of crying out to God, the lady told me to shout, "I love you Jesus!" And I did. After my third time, my mouth trembled, and God's Spirit entered my soul. I began to speak in a language I could not understand, but I wasn't trying to figure out what had just happened. The Book of Acts experience had come to life, and it was absolutely incredible.

...Repent and be baptized, every one of you in the name of Jesus Christ for the remission of sins, and ye shall receive the gift of the Holy Ghost.
Acts 2:38

I felt as if I had just captured the first place trophy at Nationals for cross-county. I was totally free. Although my body was weak, I could not leave this security. Blankets of distress and pain were being ripped from my life. I fell to my knees again, and my soul smiled with joy. A week later, *our* youth group visited the Coltharp's church in Aurora, Illinois. In the middle of the service, the Lord revealed to me that I needed to be baptized in the name of Jesus Christ. We were standing at the altar when I boldly declared that "I must be baptized!" And I was. I spoke in tongues the whole way down into the water. I could feel my soul being cleansed from sin, shame, and pain.

...Unto what then were ye baptized?
And they said, Unto John's baptism.
Then said Paul, John verily baptized with the baptism of repentance, saying unto the people, that they should believe on him which should come after him, that is, on Christ Jesus.

When they heard this, they were baptized in the name of Jesus.
Acts 19:3-5

I went home that night as a Christian, ready to tell everyone of the joy that was possible to obtain. As I walked into our dimly lit apartment, through the thick cloud of cigarette smoke, the scent of alcohol singed my nostrils, but its darkness couldn't affect my mood. I detested everything about my mom's lifestyle and the despair it brought into our lives, but this time, I refused to walk by her without a word. Instead, I stopped at the kitchen table, told her that I loved her, and began to paint the picture of all that I had experienced in the past week. Mom sat in unbelief, and in her drunken state, she urged me never to go back. Anger rushed through my veins, and I wanted to lash out at her. For the first time in my life, I was on a spiritual journey that would help heal all the hurts for which she had made contribution in my life, and she recommended I stay away from there. She mocked me and called our church a cult. Her blatant disapproval just added to my lifetime of hurt, but I told myself that night that I would pray my mom into heaven if it was the last thing I ever did. This seemed an impossible feat. She was an unhappy person who had lived a vile lifestyle for a very long time. She did not care for religious people, and she had no use for anything they had to say. However, in that same moment, I was surprised that she could quote scripture word for word.

It had been years since Vicky and I attended the after-school Awana Club, which was a form of outreach similar to church. I suddenly recollected a time that we were encouraged to memorize scripture to recite on our next visit. While trying to quote to Mom, who was of course drunk at the time, she began pounding the palm of her hand on the table and spouting off scripture. She followed up with a string of cuss words and said, "If you're going to quote the Bible, you better get it right." I later found out that Mom had been exposed to church, so I asked her why she had never talked about God or taken us to church before. She had no answers.

...goals allow you to take control. Instead of living by chance, you live by choice.
Kam Knight, Goal Setting

Entering the Real Race

Wherefore seeing we also are compassed about with so great a cloud
of witnesses, let us lay aside every weight, and the sin
which doth so easily beset us, and let us run with patience
the race that is set before us,
Hebrews 12:1

After my salvation experience, I instantly knew why God had drawn me to Janice. She was a girl who needed the Lord as much as I did, and I was sure that He would be the one who could help her. So, I brought her to church. She felt welcome there and would come as often as she was allowed. Her parents kept her in most of the time, so one day I went over to meet them and asked if she could spend the night with me on Saturday. To Janice's surprise, they said, "Yes."

Janice had lost a good portion of her hearing, so when I spoke with her, I had to face her so she could read my lips. The night she stayed with me, my sister Wendy needed a babysitter, so we went to her apartment and watched the boys until they fell asleep. Before bed, I asked Janice if she believed God could heal her hearing. She said, "Yes, I believe." I prayed a prayer of faith over her, and she instantly said she could hear. I believed her, but at the same time, I was surprised. I knew we had prayed, and I'd been reading of miracles in the Bible, but what had just happened? I really questioned.

…he gave them power…to heal all manner of sickness
and all manner of disease.
Matthew 10:1

"What song is playing on the radio?" I asked.

She replied, "Make it Right, Fall in Love with Jesus Tonight." And she was correct. We cried, rejoiced, jumped, and shouted for joy in the room! Janice went to the doctor the following Monday and was told that she had regained forty percent of her hearing. That was the first of many miracles I would begin to witness in my new walk with God. I spent my days listening to songs by Mickey Mangun, and I loved to read books written by Vesta Mangun and other great authors of our faith. I was on fire, and I was hungry for their faith and their power in prayer!

I invited every friend to church, and everyone came at one time or another. I was not ashamed of the gospel of Jesus Christ. This new-birth experience was transforming my life, and I felt an obligation and responsibility to tell the world. Janice was one of many who received the Holy Ghost and was baptized in Jesus' name. Dwayne was another. He was captain of the boys' track team and interested in me, so I brought him to church, along with many more, including Tonya, and Holly, and so many others who visited out of sheer shock at my transformation. Instead of inviting them to parties, where we drank too much and acted foolishly, we were now filling the pews during Friday night youth services.

I had the best youth group on the planet! We'd go bowling and stay up all night long praying; then we would head to a nearby restaurant for breakfast. One time, we decided to circle the outside of my house, marching around it in prayer, as if marching around the walls of Jericho. It was very spiritual until we woke the neighbors who came out yelling at us, threatening to call the police. Another time, the boys in the youth group decided to teach me to drive. It was painful sitting in Jason's living room, having to tell his parents that I'd run into a brand new Audi. I didn't even have a permit. The Audi driver was kind enough not to call the police, and

Jason's parents took it better than I expected, thankful that we were alive and nobody was seriously hurt.

On December 15, 1988, I sat on a kitchen chair and talked to Jason for hours. He was my closest friend. We were raised entirely differently, and both of us were somewhat fascinated by those differences. He had lived his entire life with Christian parents and knew only stability. My life was a wild ride that Jason could not comprehend, so he often asked me questions about my life previous to God. For some reason, I confided in him and trusted him, though our lives were worlds apart.

Often it isn't the initiating trauma that creates seemingly insurmountable pain, but the lack of support after.
S. Kelley Harrell

Hurt Chose Me Again

Mom was gone again, and as always, I was afraid of being home alone. The phone became a lifeline until I was good and ready to go to sleep. That night, I was talking about going on a mission trip and considering all the plans God might have for me. Finally, I said goodnight, hung up the phone, brushed my teeth, talked to Jesus, and fell into bed with a thousand thoughts of God's plans on my mind. I had drifted off to sleep in my favorite gown as a small amount of light peered in through a window above the bed. Approximately thirty minutes later, at 12:05 in the morning, a man entered my room, and I instantly sat straight up in fright. He had what appeared to be a thin mustache, leathery skin, evil eyes, and a deep voice. He lunged down on me and said, "Don't you move. I have a knife, and I will kill you." I was paralyzed in fear and helplessly lay there in terror. Once he finished raping me, he rolled me over and said "I'm going to sit in your mom's room, so don't you move." At this point in my life, God had performed many miracles for me. I had been healed from a good portion of my childhood trauma by staying close to God through constant worship, prayer, and reading the Word. My whole outlook on life had changed. God had given me my break in life. But now, my season of joy was abruptly interrupted. Once again, hurt chose me.

I shook in fear for my life and wondered what was going to happen next. "Was my mom home? Was this stranger going to hurt her as well? Would I die tonight?" Then I heard the door open, but it did not close. "Was he gone?" I wondered. I waited several minutes and then had to go and see. I came out of my room, turned to my right, and saw the front door entrance to the apartment was open. I ran to the kitchen phone, but he had cut the wire. Immediately, I rushed out the door and began frantically knocking on a neighbor's door, asking them to call the police.

I went back to my house to use the restroom because my bladder felt like it was going to explode. After using the toilet, I collapsed onto the floor. The next thing I knew, an emergency medical team and police arrived, and I was being taken to the hospital on a stretcher in the back of an ambulance. Within seconds, they were firing off questions to me, and instead of being treated as a victim, I felt afraid, almost like a criminal.

Soon, we arrived at the hospital, and I was taken to the emergency room. They did all of the medical things, which were painful and frightening. The police asked if I had any idea who could have done this to me. I said no, but they pushed for more. "Are you sure? You can think of no one who would have access to your door or who would know your mom would not be home?" It seemed they were demanding an explanation from me. They wanted me to tell them who committed this crime in the night. The only person I could think of who could have known I was home alone, was the man Mom had recently started dating while Klaus was away, so I mentioned his name to the police. I wasn't trying to get him into trouble. I barely knew the guy. Anything was possible.

Because I named Mom's new *acquaintance* as a possible suspect, she became nervous and feared Klaus would find out she had been cheating on him. She rejected me instead of believing me and threw me out of the house. I wanted to hide under a thousand blankets and cry out to the only One who saw this crime and knew my pain. At times, the agony of what had transpired was unrelenting. It was worse than the instant stripping away of my self-worth. It was the rejection I suffered from Mom, who knew everything, and chose not to spare me. I wanted my Heavenly Father to wrap His arms around me and hold me tightly while assuring me that this was one more thing I could endure.

The pain I suffered did not instantly go away. I looked over my shoulder for many years to come. The night it happened, I was sleeping on my back, something I have never done since. Though several close friends and family members hurt for me, and even questioned how God could allow this additional misfortune to come my way, I never questioned it. I knew I did not deserve it, but hurt had chosen me, and in its occurrence, I found a depth in the Lord on a level I could not have otherwise known. Without this level of deep hurt, I may not have reached that greater place of *seeking* God. The fear of men would remain with me a very long time. It was to some degree inescapable, but the depth I found in God kept the enemy from taking away my inner joy and peace of mind. During my anguish, I was able to dig deeper and find a hidden place in God I had no idea existed. God was not the enemy. He was not at fault. The Lord was my Redeemer. My Comforter. He became my mother, who couldn't love me like a child needed to be loved. He became my absentee father. Jesus was all that I had.

In those aching months to come, I discovered that with God, I could survive anything that came my way. I had already been attending Canaan Apostolic for ten months, so the church was invested in my life. When they found out that I was not only a victim of rape, but also now homeless, they were not about to turn their backs on me. Bro. and Sis. Hood sat down with me and talked about a place called Tupelo Children's Mansion that helped young people in times like this. It sounded like a nice option. Even though it was far away in a state I'd never visited, I was not opposed to going. Before that time came, Connie and Jim stepped in. Connie was a piano player at our church. I had visited her home many times and thought highly of her. She could sing and play, and she treated her husband and children with love and kindness. I stayed in their home for the next six months, rooming with ten-year-old Julie. I would sleep on my side, pressed close to the inside of her twin metal bed, and hang onto the rails for the duration of the night. Lying beside her, I tried to remain as still as possible. A thousand warm, but quiet tear-drops, fell from my eyes as I relived the horror of the night that got me thrown out of my home by my mother, and tried to pray myself to sleep. It was in that little girl's room, as I suffered, that God surrounded me and assured me that His ways were not my ways, and one day, my hurt would lessen, the shame would fade, and somehow, my humiliation and loss of self-worth would have meaning.

After the rape, I could no longer focus at school. I was a semester away from graduating, and I had lost my drive. I began to distance myself from friends. I just wanted to get to graduation and move on with my life. Track season was on the horizon, but I was no longer sure I could bring myself to run.

Quizzing

Since leaving Mom's, I was living happily with Connie. I also left my McDonald's job and started working at Walgreen's. I was off that day, so I decided to attend the church's Bible Quiz meeting. Carl Morgan shared his heart as did several other adults, including Pam, Joyce and Theresa. They told us how important it was to hide the Word in our hearts, and what a difference it could make in our lives. I was desperate for a reason to walk away from track, because in light of what I'd experienced, it had lost its appeal. My decision was made. I traded my track shoes for something that would soon begin to change my life in a way that nothing else could. Taking a box of Bible Quiz cards home, I quickly began memorizing the book of Romans. Because it was already January, we were all instructed to learn chapter one. I was told to learn all of the even chapters, Dwayne was told to learn all of the odd, and Steve had to know all sixteen chapters because he was a seasoned quizzer who had the drive and could handle the load. This experience of memorizing the Word, quoting it over and over, day after day, began to heal my hurting heart. I was learning Bible stories for the first time ever and discovering all about Paul's journeys. I was learning how to fully overcome sin through scripture.

I beseech you therefore, brethren, by the mercies of God, that ye present your bodies a living sacrifice, holy, acceptable unto God, which is your reasonable service.
And be not conformed to this world: but be ye transformed by the renewing of your mind, that ye may prove what is that good, and acceptable, and perfect, will of God.
Romans 12:1-2

Though unfamiliar with the Bible, the scripture began to come alive for me. I was so hungry to be whole, and I wanted all that God had to offer. Bible Quizzing was two-fold. It wasn't

only an opportunity to memorize and diagram scripture, but it was also a highly competitive game involving deep levels of learning, self-control, discipline, and good sportsmanship. This form of learning was teaching me not only how to lead, but also how to follow. Steve was captain of our team, and he was stellar. Steve was different than any other teenager I had ever met. He was serious and purposeful. While the rest of our youth group was running around on Saturdays having fun, Steve would be studying for hours. Once I asked him what he was doing, and he said, "I need to learn eight verses today, review, and do some charting." That seemed awfully extraordinary to me. Watching his life taught me about a level of consecration I was unaware young people could develop. Dwayne, who sat in the second seat, was one of my friends from the boys' cross-country team. He loved to

run. It was his life. Because I was now a passionate Christian, telling everyone of the joy that was possible to attain, Dwayne was one of several who came into the church from my high school. Like me, he also chose to put his running shoes aside for the new sport of quizzing. We

both missed the pavement in many ways, but we saw the

78

long-term effect of quizzing, even at our young age. Bible Quizzing took us on many adventures across the states. I don't remember whether or not I was a great quizzer, although I was awarded the Novice trophy at State finals. I mostly remember Bro. Upchurch laughing every time I stood boldly to contest an answer given by someone on the opposing team. I loved to contest!

Through Bible Quizzing, our team from Roselle, Illinois, visited the headquarters of the United Pentecostal Church. While there, I heard Sis. Claudette Walker delivered a powerful message about following after Christ. Leaving the devotional, I picked up a pamphlet that read, "Don't just go to Bible College, go to Gateway College of Evangelism!" I was intrigued. It had gotten my full attention.

College Years

I wasn't sure what it meant to go to Bible College, but even as a new babe in Christ, I was a passionate soul winner. Within months, my thoughts of attending Ball State University as a Journalism major had faded. I felt a call to evangelize my world! With little more than a Bible and a suitcase, my Quiz Coach, Carl Morgan, moved me to St. Louis. I had been working at the local Walgreen's for the past year and was awarded the first ever scholarship of $1,000 in our area. I had no help from my mom or Klaus, but I brought with me a semester's worth of earnings and a whole lot of faith. I did not even know how to drive. I arrived without a rug, curtains, blankets, heater, tiny refrigerator, or even a pillow. Carl, and his fiancé, Pat, who he later married, took me to the store and bought me a pillow, along with a set of sheets for the twin size bed that was now mine. To this day, I still have peers who tease me about not knowing what hit them the day I arrived on the scene. I was ready to go door-knocking and witness. Though I knew I had much to learn, I desperately wanted to be a light to the world!

My first day of college taught me the greatest lesson I would ever learn. I was sitting in class when my teacher, Reverend Ed Lucas, made what I considered to be a snide comment directed toward me. I can't remember what he said, but I replied by telling him to "Shut up." The class fell silent. I was later called into our college President Stanley Chamber's office. He welcomed me to the school. He told me that I came to Bible College for a reason, and the first one was to learn respect for authority. Bro. Chambers talked to me for a long time, and then Bro. Lucas came in. I apologized profusely, and I left the office a changed young lady. I'd already been in church nearly two years, and they had worked diligently doing clean-up work on me, but apparently I still had a long way to go. I was okay with it. I knew I was too sensitive and had a bit of a smart mouth, so I looked forward to having Christian educators speak into my life and teach me.

Sister Anne Wilkins, my all-time favorite teacher, used to say, "Annette, you're a diamond in the rough, and God has a lot of polishing to do." I would sit in Sis. Wilkins' classes in awe of her anointed teaching and later follow her to the office with more questions. I was hungry for God and ambitious to learn. I longed for healing and for the same anointing that she and so many of my instructors possessed.

College life was everything I had ever dreamed it would be. The work was not too difficult, but not having the Biblical basics that most of my classmates possessed from having had a Christian heritage, made it a little more challenging for me. The principles and truths they had been taught all their lives, both at home and in Sunday School, became new revelations to me every day. Learning was fascinating, the extensive traveling was great, and the long talks with friends were awesome. I felt like a sponge, absorbing everything.

I did not know how to sing, but after only one semester, I was chosen to travel with the college chorale. I considered this a huge honor. When I asked our choir director what my part would be, she said, "You're an alto, but to be honest, we are bringing you to testify." I was both elated and frightened at the same time. I had no idea what she wanted me to say, but she told me not to worry because I had an anointing, and God would give me the words." And He did. Each night, I would take the microphone just before the song, "Hallowed be thy Name," and God would put His words in me every single time. I prayed, trusted Him, and allowed His anointing to flow through me. It was amazing how far I'd come. Even though I had to work forty hours a week throughout my college years, and taking the summer off work to travel was a financial sacrifice, it was a privilege to witness and pray with so many people over such a short amount of time.

Walgreen's gave me my start in college. Without their initial investment, God would have needed to open a different door. The craziest, most phenomenal thing about this miracle was, not only did I receive the prestigious scholarship, but I was also transferred to a newly-built Walgreen's within walking distance of the college. When I say it was in walking distance, I mean across the street. I not only embarked on this journey with some money, but I also had a job the day I arrived in town. I kept that job until I graduated, and most weeks, I worked thirty to forty hours. My friends often complained that I worked too much and was missing out on a lot of after-class fun, but I had no choice. My hours were 2:30 – 11:00, and I made a lot of memories in that little store.

My friends often stopped by and spoiled me with meals while visiting me on my breaks, and I soon realized that this place would become  somewhat of a missions-church for me. I walked in with a pep in my step, a scripture on my heart, and a song in my mind. Jesus went with me, and with His help, many prayers and miracles took place there. One particular time, I had been learning about fasting and decided to try doing it. I prayed often and went without food for about four days. During this fasting experience, I held a healing-line, right at the register. My co-worker Marie had back problems and walked with a hunched back. Feeling an unction in the Holy Ghost, I told her that God wanted to heal her back. If she believed that He could, it would happen right then. Marie said, "I believe. I believe in your God." I began to pray, and instantly Marie stood straight up and was healed. Afterwards, a line of customers stood one by one and asked me to pray for them. It was crazy-amazing, and because I did not care what anyone thought of me, it worked, for God's glory.

I suffered with terrible migraines in college. I took a lot of Tylenol and pushed through until one night in a Vespers prayer meeting. It was about midnight, and we were crying out to the Lord in prayer. While I lay there I said, "Lord, my migraines are preventing me from doing a great work for you. If you will heal me, I will give you the praise and testify of your grace." Instantly, my headache was gone, and it never returned.

Money was tight, and I had already received a few notices that time was up. Though I was close to our school leadership, paying our tuition was not optional. My friend Krystal stopped by my room one morning and said, "I believe our time is up, I'm going to pack."

I asked her, "What are you talking about?" She proceeded to hand me a letter that said my payment had to be forthcoming, or I would have to leave the school. I dismissed the letter and fell to my knees. I prayed, "Lord, you called me to Bible College, and I know that your calling is still present with me. You see how hard I'm working and you know that I have nothing more to give. Please pay my bill today." It was that simple. I did not cry. I never begged. I gave Him the facts and placed it in His hands.

After my simple prayer, I got up from the floor and proceeded to fill my hair with hot-sticks. No sooner than my hot curlers were in, the phone rang. It was still early, but a few classes were in session and Sis. Monfort was already in her office. I heard a friend outside my room calling to me. I was needed on the phone. I walked down the hall in faith, thanking God for what He was about to do. And here it came. Sis. Monfort said, "Annette, I don't know how this happened, but someone just paid your tuition bill in full."

"Really?" I exclaimed, "Wow! For the entire month?"

Sis. Monfort replied in astonishment, "No, for the year!" I went to class beaming because the scripture I was learning was absolute truth, and had just become absolutely real to me.

But my God shall supply all your need
according to His riches in glory by Christ Jesus.
Philippians 4:19

Another miracle that took place occurred in the summer of 1992. I had gone on puppet-tour for two weeks, followed by a mission trip to Dover Foxcroft, Maine. While there, we knocked on doors, taught Bible studies, led worship services, and encouraged the pastor's family in their new work. It was an incredible week that provided me with a lifetime friend, Judy Dillard, and a host of memories. I returned to college on a spiritual high, but flat broke. I was staying on campus for the summer, so I used what little money I had in the bank to pay my rent. I had two freezer-burnt pot pies and a pack of Ramen noodles to last about a week before I would get paid again. I knew I could find a few after-church dates who would probably pay for dinner, but I also felt like I was headed for a lengthy fast unless God intervened. So, I went back to the prayer room. While there, I may have cried some, but my request was simple. "God, you know my heart and you see my need. Please provide manna from heaven to feed me. I don't want to tell anyone I have a need when I know you're enough to supply it." About four hours later, my miracle came. Someone from the end of the hallway was calling my name. They said I had two huge boxes at the bottom of the stairs that had just arrived in the mail. I asked them to please bring them up to my room. I quickly saw that these were addressed from my mom. That in itself was strange. In three years, she had never sent me a package. I did not think she even knew the college address. I opened the boxes, and I was in complete shock. I believed when I prayed my prayer, but this was insanely ridiculous. The boxes were packed with enough food to last me through the summer. They contained cases of tuna fish, large packs of Ramen noodles, boxed cereal, macaroni and cheese, and a super-sized bag of gummy bears, just to name a few of the things. I went straight to the phone and called Mom.

I had not talked to my mother in several weeks. In mid-May, she had let me know that she preferred I not come home for the summer, and I was hurt. I had to scramble to find the funds to pay rent for June and July, and it was also a little late to be asking to stay for the summer. Our dorms had no air-conditioning, and I was sad about missing out on spending a glorious eight weeks with my Chicago youth group. Still, the boxes were here, and a call had to be made. Mom answered in her regularly gruff voice, and I started talking. "Hey Mom, it's Sam! I just got the boxes, and I am so happy. I just can't believe you did this. These packages came just in time." The phone was silent. "Mom, are you there?"

85

"Yes, I'm here, but what are you talking about? What packages?"

I answered, "The boxes of food you sent me! It's a miracle, Mom. I got up around 6 AM this morning and cried out to God for provision. He used you to supply my need. I have no money or food and had no idea what I was going to do to eat."

Mom said in disbelief, "Tell me what's in the boxes."

"Okay," and I started rattling off what had come in the boxes. "Tuna fish, Ramen noodles and my favorite gummy bears." And the list went on.

Mom still thought I was lying. She said, "Tell me more." I literally went through the entire contents of both boxes, giving her a detailed account of all that was in them. Afterwards, she began to cry.

I was puzzled. "Mom, are you okay? I don't understand. What is wrong? I just called to say thank you."

Her response sent chills throughout my body, and I sat in absolute astonishment. Mom said, "Sam, I believe you, but I just don't understand. I went to the post office this morning. Those boxes were mailed four hours ago. I don't understand how this is even possible."

> *But Jesus … said unto them, With men this is impossible;*
> *but with God all things are possible.*
> **Matthew 19:26**

That miracle was a building block that changed our lives. It provided healing for me because it gave me faith that my mom still loved me, and that I was on her mind. It also let me know that as long as I was walking in His ways, no matter the circumstances, God would never allow me to go hungry. For

Mom, it planted a seed of faith in her heart that would continue to grow in the years to come. Though I have endless memories of travel, friendships and fundraising, it is the teaching, training, and depth in prayer that has kept me all these years. God performed many great works and miracles for me and through me during this season of my life, proving to me over and over again, just how real He is. I held onto this reality and built from the lessons I learned.

Bible College was a spiritual journey where I learned abundantly, but it wasn't all prayer meetings, evangelism and study. Karen, Angelique, Robyn, Ann and I would stay up all night laughing and talking. When it came time for room inspections, I would stand boldly on my bed and shout, "Room, be cleaned this instant, in Jesus name!" I'd entertain them with songs as I jumped on the bed, carrying on about my current crush. This was gloriously fun until the time I fell off the bed and my arm came out of socket. Laughter turned to screaming and the entire floor was in my room. Every day was an adventure.

Graduation was quickly approaching, and like most of my classmates, I was nervous and anxious. I loved college life. I loved learning in class and traveling the states, evangelizing. We had incredible chapel services. I had built strong friendships with my peers, so saying goodbye was difficult. Knowing where to go next was even more difficult.

At the time, I was attending Bro. Urshan's church in St. Peter's, Missouri. Their assembly had become like family to me, and the thought of leaving would be tough. I was especially close to Jim and Janice Peters and their daughter, Tracy. They were my Bible College family. Bro. Urshan also felt bad about my departure and offered me a position as his secretary. That sounded good, but it wasn't grand enough for me. I was hoping for a foreign country or a Home Mission's church in a town I never heard of except by revelation from God.

A few months earlier, I had attended the United Pentecostal Church General Conference in Salt Lake City to minister in the children's church with our college puppet-team. It was a long and treacherous trip across the country. To entertain ourselves, we teasingly tortured  Brother McDougal the whole way there. He had not worked for the school long and was serving as our Vice President at the time. He was Canadian. I'm not certain what I did to earn the attention, but he loved getting me riled. While in Utah, I met several missionaries and was sure to put a little money in each of their baskets as I walked by their booths. I loved hearing their stories and was in tears while they talked.

At that same conference, I stopped by the Tupelo Children's Mansion booth. This was intriguing to me since it had only been about five years earlier that it could have been my home. After viewing the Mansion's video presentation, which was quite interesting in itself, Eric Burton walked up to shake my hand. "Hi. I'm Eric, and I just got adopted. I'm from Tupelo Children's Mansion." I was smitten by Eric's self-confidence and kindness, and I wanted to hear all about him and this wonderful place that he said had raised him. He talked about living on a wide-open campus with a bunch of brothers and sisters. He was a delightful young man with a wonderful attitude.

Eric remained in my thoughts even after General Conference. I wondered how old he was, and what it must have been like to have lived in the same place for so long. I never felt sorry for him. I thought he was lucky, because whatever was happening at the children's home seemed to have made a huge impact on his life. In the next few weeks, I continued praying until the answer came. I did not understand how it could have happened, but a letter came to me from one of the Directors at the Mansion. I had no idea how they had gotten my name and address. I did not leave it with Eric. In the meantime, someone from home told me that my friend, Pam, was working there and loved it. I was also told that Jeff and Nadeen, a young couple who were friends from Gateway, were there. Without so much as a thought of what position I would hold or what the pay would be, I could feel the tug. It was God confirming to me that He knew my name and had a plan for my future. I found my mission field, nestled in the quaint little town of Tupelo, Mississippi.

Finding my Mission Field

When I first moved to Mississippi, it did not feel big enough. I knew God was directing me, but at the same time, it was worlds away from all I had envisioned. I was thinking, "What do you mean, God? I'm not going to Africa? You're not going to call me to Missions? After all, I did just dedicate years of my life to study at a place called Gateway College of Evangelism."

Though the finality of this move still remained a mystery to me, it did not take long to discover how the unfolding of my own story of losses, rejection, homelessness, hurt, and abuse would in time help impact children who were finding shelter from their storms at Tupelo Children's Mansion. The puzzle pieces were coming together.

I was class President in college, so my move to Tupelo was instantly humbling. I was no longer a big fish, but a small minnow in a great big pond. The sprawling campus felt like a town all its own, and I wondered how long it would take to learn the names of all the children, not to mention finding my way around the school-grounds. My first day of work was rough. For starters, in the daily morning prayer meeting, when Bro. Tom Velie mentioned that the AP was one-hundred-thousand dollars in the red, I responded with a hearty, "Praise the Lord!" My boss nudged me and said, "Annette, that's money we owe." Later, I was introduced to a very common Southern tradition of etiquette by Sis. Baker who ran the kitchen. Standing in line for my first meal, she asked, "Green beans?" I replied, "Yea." She asked again and again as if she had not heard me the first time or any other time. So, I repeated myself, "Yes, I will take some." She looked at me with a smile and said, "Honey, around here it's 'Yes, ma'am,' or you don't get served." Being from Chicago, this was new to me!

I had learned a little about photography in college, but not enough to begin a career path in the field. Yet, I was soon handed a camera that was heavier than my purse with a box of film and a long list of children  who needed photographing. On top of this, I was given a huge map with instructions to begin planning tours across the United States, Mexico, and Canada, where the children would travel to designated church destinations and sing. I was twenty-two years old and still couldn't even drive. Even though I had traveled the country as a child, I'd never learned to read a map. I was told that I was going to be a communications assistant, which entailed giving campus tours and doing a lot of writing.

Gwen Dillon was my new boss, and we grew close quickly. She was an amazing lady who taught me the Mansion ropes. She said it was my job to meet with visiting sponsors, show them around the campus, and introduce them to children and staff members. I would compose letters about the children and mail them to their sponsors, letting them know how their child was doing emotionally, physically, and spiritually. At the time, it did not seem like all of those jobs had a lot to do with my college degree, but I adapted quickly and fell in love with every aspect of my position. All of this was exciting, and I learned quickly.

The first little girl I met was Candi. She was a beautiful, brown-haired charmer who had me wrapped around her finger from the minute I met her. She looked me in the eyes, and without hesitation, began telling me a little about her story. I sat in shock! Next, I met Kathy for an interview and photo session. She was another child who held my heart within minutes. Then there was Erica. This beautiful young girl put on a tough act, but I could see right through it. I met Rebecca, Nellie, Amber, Jason, Nicky, Michael, Jordan, and the list went on and on. I could not believe that I was actually learning their names, but also a part of their stories. At times, the teenagers gave me a run for my money because I was young, single and close to their age. Eventually, I gained their trust and soon began to minister to them with great ease. Before this adventure, I knew there was great suffering in the world. After all, I was a product of it. But, I had no idea that it was so broad and vast. Here I was, swimming in a sea of children raised similar to me.

One by one, I met them. I interviewed them, and I cried in my secret place over their hurts. In some ways, this new job called ministry, peeled back old Band-Aids from wounds I'd forgotten were there. I knew what God had done for me, and though much of the pain was suppressed, I was reminded how He had turned my life around for His glory, and given me hope and a future. Because of this, I could see that our labor in Tupelo would not be in vain. I also knew those kids' healing would take time, love, and even more time. Every once in a while, one of their stories would trigger memories from my past, and I would go running back to my Jesus that night to thank Him, for not only saving me, but also for bringing me to a place where I could make a difference.

I was not hired to teach, nor was I called to be a social worker. The kids were my calling, but fundraising was my gift. I wanted to be with the children all the time, but I knew I had a special talent with people. I came to realize that God needed me to help the children by getting to know the people who helped keep them at the Mansion.

I loved going to work, and I heard the phone ringing before I could even get the door unlocked. Inevitably, if I missed them, they would call right back. "Thank you for calling Tupelo Children's Mansion. How may I help you?" And my day would begin. The calls ranged from wanting to know if their Special Kid had received his gift to a need for prayer for a dying spouse. Some called just to talk. They wanted to share their lives with someone, and I was becoming a good listener. One day, my boss said I chatted a bit too much and needed to find a way to curtail the calls to at least ten minutes. It took time, but I eventually got the hang of it. I began to feel connected to donors from unfamiliar towns and states I had never visited. It was fascinating! Many are now among our closest friends.

Deciding to Love

It was in May of 1995 when Robert first walked onto the Tupelo Children's Mansion Campus. He was a former Army guy who was the back-of-the-house manager at the newly-opened Outback Steakhouse. He had hired a few of the children associated with TCM (Tupelo Children's Mansion) and was soon invited to attend our services. Robert was tall with broad shoulders and a firm handshake. He was quiet and reserved, but he had a strength about him. The first time I laid eyes on him, he was sitting staunchly on the back row and looked as if he was in the mafia. He did not make a move or even crack a smile. The first service kind of shocked him, but he said he enjoyed it. He had not gone to church much in his life and wasn't used to people expressing themselves in the Pentecostal manner. He repented in January of 1996 and received the Holy Ghost six months later.

Robert was quiet but also very kind. For the first year he attended services, I noticed him from time to time, but I spoke to him very little. I was dating a youth pastor from Missouri and had no thoughts of the single men in our church. Besides, Robert was too new in the church. However, after a while, we started to run around together, strictly as friends. He was very helpful to me, and I began to really enjoy his company. Whatever needed to be done, he was there to do it. He ran errands with me and for me, helped me paint my on-campus house, taught me how to drive, and came to play board games with all the singles at my house.

On Valentine's Day, Robert brought me roses, yet I still considered him just a great friend. There were a few girls on campus who liked him, and I urged him to date them. Robert was a great listener. I would talk to him for hours about the man I thought I loved and ask him for his input. He would quietly listen and give me sound advice when I finished. Then one day, things shifted. We were on a youth trip to Hot Springs, Arkansas, when it happened. Our youth committee had taken the young people to a prayer conference. Standing outside on the left of a building, Robert shocked me when he said, "I know you and I are really good friends, but I was just curious if you would be interested in going out with me on a date next week?" I was flabbergasted. Why was he ruining our great friendship? I couldn't believe my ears.

Without even thinking, I blurted out, "No, I will not go out with you. I'm sorry but I don't like you in that way. I just want to remain good friends." Ugh! This was the worst, and I felt terrible.

Robert surprised me by his calm response. He was confident and well poised. He did not seem shocked or even disappointed by my words. This impressed me. He looked me in the eyes and confidently replied, "No problem and don't worry, I will not ask twice." Wow. This was new. This felt different. For some reason, I expected him to fall apart or seem sad, but no, he held it together and appeared unfazed by our exchange. I did not think any more about this and told no one. The last thing I wanted was to be pressured into liking someone who I only saw as a friend, and I certainly did not want it talked about amongst the others. This was in January 1997.

Robert and I remained friends. We continued to talk, go on walks, cook together, and enjoy one another's company. He had several girls liking him, and we would discuss his options, all while I shared my dating drama. We were quite the pair. Meanwhile, others began to notice how often I referred to Robert. My Mom even said, "Are you sure you don't have feelings for that man? You talk about him every time I hear from you." I was offended and shocked that she even asked. I would always insist that she was crazy.

It was a warm day in May, and I was driving to the photo lab where I always had our pictures developed. I was frustrated and hurt over a young man I'd finally broken up with a few months earlier. He had written me a letter and was trying to work things out with me. I had really fallen for him, but he was too demanding. Every phone call felt more like a job interview. I was never able to be myself, never felt like I was enough. It was so complicated and problematic. He would write pages of questions for me, and I always felt like I was getting the answers wrong. I felt small in his presence, and even though I was drawn to him, I knew God could not possibly want this for me.

A few days after deciding not to allow that relationship to rekindle, I was excited to meet all of the singles at Woody's restaurant for an all-you-can eat seafood dinner. Everyone had been talking about this for days, and it sounded like a fantastic plan. At the last minute, my roommates decided not to go, so I decided to ride with Robert. It was not a date. We were just two friends headed to the same restaurant. We arrived on time, but no one else came. This was before everyone owned cell phones, so we had no way of calling to see why none of the others had come. We decided to go in and have dinner.

The place was beautiful. Our table was covered in a linen cloth, located near a window. The lights were dim, and the food was divine. We talked, and laughed, and thoroughly enjoyed the evening. When the waitress brought our tickets, Robert grabbed mine and said, "Please, let me pay, just this once." I agreed, feeling I had been blessed by a friend. That night as we traveled home, Robert said something that sent a chill down my arm. The car was quiet, and we were comfortably driving down Main Street when he turned and said, "You know, you are really quite beautiful."

I was flattered, and those words stayed with me. I said, "Thank you," with a smile, and we began chatting about the weather.

The next day it hit me. I was brought back to a conversation I once had with President Tim Dugas in Bible College. I was the girl who was always in search of God's perfect will. I was the one who always talked myself out of relationships, and always blamed God for the outcome. Bro. Dugas had told me that I made things way too complicated, and that when it came right down to it, love was a decision. He said that one day I would have to finally let down my guard and choose to love and be loved. I could barely hold the steering wheel or see out the window because I began to weep.

I cried out to God. "Lord, have I missed the boat entirely? Is Robert the man for me? Is he the one you designed for my life?" I could hardly believe I was saying these words out loud. Did I already love this man? Had I fallen for my best friend? Could he be the one? I remembered that Robert had told me he would never ask me out again, so I prayed a prayer. "God, if he is the one that I should not only date, but also marry, have him ask me out again. I know he said he would never ask me twice, so soften his heart toward me and show him your will." And that day, it happened. I was at work, and it was around 3:00 PM when the call came.

"Hey, what are you doing tonight? I was thinking about making chicken bowtie pasta with a yogurt sauce and wanted to see if you would come for dinner?"

What? I could not believe my ears. I'd never been to his apartment, but I said yes. I was scared. I told no one. I wanted to make sure this was all really happening. Was I falling for the boy who literally lived next door? The one I said I would never date?

That night was amazing. For some reason, I saw him in an entirely new light. I walked in hoping to feel nothing, but that did not happen. I saw him as a different person. We ate, and talked, and I felt a lightness in the air. It dawned on me just how much I loved being with this person. I came to realize that he was the person I thought about each morning when I awoke and each night as I went to sleep. I reminisced over all of the fun things we had shared. I felt absolutely comfortable around him. I was loud and outgoing, and Robert's presence brought calmness to my life. My energy and flair put pep in his step and brought a joy to his day. His kindness gave me pause, and my quick wit made him laugh. We completed one another. That night, out of the blue, Robert reached over and kissed me on the cheek. I was stunned! I turned to him, and he said, "Why can't you just admit that you're crazy about me? About us." What? Wow! This was really happening. He was right. I was crazy about him and about us.

I went back to my house and talked to Karen and Paula. They had been my roommates for three years and had lived through my friendship with Robert. I told them to sit down because I needed to share something with them. "I love Robert Tomlinson, and I'm going to marry him."

What? They were absolutely stunned! I am positive that Karen fell on the ground laughing, and Paula sat there in shock. Karen and I spent four years in college together before we both decided to move to Tupelo. She knew me well. She had lived through many relationships with me and could not believe her ears. We talked for hours and hours that night. I was on an emotional high. I knew I had found Mr. Right.

The next day Robert asked me to attend the Tupelo Christian Academy banquet with him, and I gleefully accepted. It was a wonderful evening, and I felt as if I was floating on air. Our secret was out, and we did not care if everyone knew it. We were a couple. After the banquet, he came to the house and as we stood outside in the darkness of night, he said, "I love you. I know that I love you." From there, we went inside and talked.

"Robert," I said, "I was once told by a very wise man that love is a decision. And I have made mine. I love you too. And I want to marry you."

Robert was floored. He said, "Are you serious? Are you asking me to marry you?"

"No, absolutely not!" I exclaimed back to him. "You need a ring, and I want a grand proposal. I have no idea what it should be, but it has to wow me. However, I do promise to say yes!" And just like that, we were planning a wedding, two dates into our *official* courtship.

Robert went the following day to meet with Pastor. He told Bro. Drury that he loved me and wanted to ask me to marry him. Bro. Drury said, "Robert, I know you love her, and I know it is God's perfect will for you to marry her. What took you so long?" And, Robert began to make his plans.

About two weeks later, Robert and I were invited to Jenny and Lisa's house for a surprise birthday party for our friend Larry. When we walked in, it was me who was given the surprise of a lifetime. All of my friends shouted, "Surprise!" Robert took a ring off the cake, knelt in front of me and proposed. I was stunned! Of course, I said, "Yes!" I was pleased with his ability to pull off such an exciting event without my knowledge. From that moment on, we spent every moment planning the wedding of my dreams!

Annette's Parents

One question I have been asked often over the years is how I transitioned my years of abuse, much of which was sexual, into a wholesome, Godly marriage. I feel it only right to address this. I was seventeen at the time of my salvation. I had experienced rape before and after coming to Christ, as well as other forms of sexual abuse throughout the years. In spite of all this, when salvation came, so did my healing. I understand that years of abuse and pain are not so easily erased for all, but for me, much of it was instant. When the Holy Spirit came into my life, He took my brokenness, pain, and shame, and literally began to remake me. After coming to Christ, I also promised the Lord and myself that I would never again make the conscious decision to engage in sexual activities outside of marriage. I kept that promise to myself. By the time I married nearly ten years later, it was as if I was pure again. I had kept myself all those years, and God had made me a wholesome, Godly, young woman, of whom I believe He and I were both proud. I don't share that to brag, but to say that redemption is available for all and any who want it.

This book tells parts of my story, but much is withheld. Unsaid. Unwritten so as not to embarrass me, Mom, or those who robbed me significantly of my youth. I wanted to allow you to have a glimpse into my world, but I also believe that much is forgiven and is under the blood. Like Pastor Judd has always taught me, there are some things that can be left unsaid. The powerful truth is, God came and knocked at the door of my heart, and I answered His knock. His healing sometimes came through testing. I was a teenage wreck, but His people were righteous and loved me through to the other side. I was a girl who wanted more than the cruel life I had been handed. God's people stepped in and helped me transition from a broken girl to a whole woman. Being raised in an unstable, often abusive, and reckless home, left me with few answers on how to live above my upbringing. His people, my church family, modeled what it was to have a Godly marriage, become a praying parent, and show respect to a new husband. Those simple things were as challenging for me to learn as chemistry was in school. Through studying the Word, following my mentors, and desiring only the best of what God could do with my life, He molded me year after year into the Christian wife and mother I was meant to be. At times, I have failed Him, but He has never one time failed me.

The Lord has blessed our marriage. He has given us three beautiful children, and it is my greatest honor to be their mom. He has also enriched our lives with grandchildren. As we move into the second part of this book, you will see that I have not chosen to share intimate details about our home life, as I have chosen to reserve it for a future book. What I have chosen to reveal instead, are my answers to the pain and hurt I endured. We have broken a generational curse of abandonment, abuse, and neglect. The keys to healing are in *My Answers to Hurt.*

Part 2

My Answers to Hurt

... the mark of a true mentor: a leader who creates a culture of excellence, and whose confidence in us makes us better than we ever dreamed we could be.
The Fine Art of Tough Love, K. Anders Ericsson, Michael J. Prietula, Edward T. Cokely Less

Mentors in my Life

When I first became saved, no one gave a seminar on the importance of mentors in your life. In fact, it was a word I seldom heard. Wandering aimlessly through life, and traveling down many roads and highways with no purpose, was no longer my path or direction. I wanted my life to have meaning and significance. I desired health, wholeness, and the ability to invest in others.

I carried the pieces of my shattered childhood and the battle scars of my past. I was now gloriously healed through His grace and was anointed to preach and teach, through the word of my testimony and example of my life. But, I needed more than just those things. To truly become the woman of God I knew I was called to be, I would need mentors to guide and lead me. I watched friends and leaders whose lives exemplified Christ in everything they did and said, leaders who not only taught the Word of God but also modeled it.

As a teenager, I followed Martha, my youth pastor's wife. She was a newlywed, but more importantly, she was a prayer warrior who had been raised in a pastor's home. Associating with her taught me plenty. I knew very early that I wanted my life to look like hers. From her, I learned how to pray, and I allowed her to influence my life. Martha showed me what it was to sacrifice, to give, and to serve. She and Mark had little when they first married, but all that they had, they shared. I spent a year under their leadership before heading to Bible College, and I tucked away their training for my future.

In Bible College, God gifted me with a teacher who saw my sincere love for Christ, and knew that I had potential. Sis. Anne Wilkins pushed me arduously. Not only did she expect me to live above reproach at all cost, but she also expected excellence inside and out of the classroom. Under her training, I became the editor of the yearbook, and let us just say, that task was often grueling. I would write a story, and she would ask me that dreaded question before even taking it out of my hands, "Is this your best, Annette?" She forced me to think and rethink, often sending me back to the drawing board.

"I believe it is my best," I would usually say, and she would give me the *look*. Oh, how I hated that *look*!

She would stare into my eyes as if seeing straight into my heart, and she would ask again, "Are you handing me your best work, or could it be cleaned a little more?" Ugh! I would take the paper back and reread it, polishing it, just like she and God were continuously polishing me. Sis. Wilkins was my mentor. Allowing her to teach me did not always mean I heard what I wanted to hear; it meant I was giving her permission to make me a better person.

Other mentors from Bible College included Janice Peters, my adopted "mom," and Pastor Johnathan Urshan, who I sat under while attending Gateway College for four years.

Once I married, my two mentors became my boss, Sonya Laughlin, and my dear friend Terri Anderson, who also worked at the Mansion. Oh how much these two ladies taught me.

I would sit in awe as I watched Sonya model what it was to keep a tidy home, cook gourmet meals, and take care of her family. She was the ultimate Martha Stewart of the church, and I wanted to usher into my home the same peace and serenity that she had in her home. Sonya and I talked daily. I knew what she was cooking, what trials she was currently facing, and how she would overcome. She taught me that it was my role and duty as a wife to respect Robert, even when I did not agree with him. She taught me about the usefulness of cooking with herbs and spices, and bringing my best to the table I set for my family. Lowering my voice with my children would be much more powerful than raising it. I have lived everything she modeled, and it has served me well.

Terri and I bonded instantly after I came to the Mansion. We shared a love for souls and for prayer. We would spend hours in prayer, learning more about prayer, and teaching the children of Tupelo Children's Mansion to do the same. She was and still is a prayer warrior in my eyes. Terri also taught me the most powerful lesson I think someone in ministry can know, and that is the importance and power of guarding your heart. Through hours of counsel, two decades of friendship, and many trials, I lived and learned this truth from my dear friend. With ministry comes much pain, because people are just people, and no matter how much they love God, good people sometimes hurt other good people. You don't serve over two decades in Kingdom service and not witness these truths. So many times, especially in my younger years, I saw things I did not understand, like decisions made, or Christian leaders falling. Hurt, pain, and wounds occur within the church, and until we fully grasp that, our ability to be used fully will fall short. There have been numerous times throughout my service at the Mansion that I leaned on Terri's wisdom and knowledge. In every circumstance, she has led me to scripture, sharing truths found in His Word. She has taught me to love, forgive, pray, fast, and guard my heart. We have both lost family members due to suicide. There is nothing more crushing, or more painful and brutal to bear, but because Terri had already walked this road, she was beside me every step of the way during this trying time in my life, helping me through my pain. Everyone needs a Terri. If you don't have one, find one. You need a mentor who can breathe life into you when the waters get muddy and you need to see more clearly.

Pastor Stephen Judd has been my mentor in ministry and in business. He has pushed me, encouraged me, and believed in me when I did not even believe in myself. His level of leadership is unlike any other I have seen. I connect with his type-A personality as mine is similar in many regards. Like Sis. Wilkins, Pastor has modeled nothing short of excellence. He does everything the right way, instead of taking the easy path. His life has modeled righteousness, and above all else, he believes in truth. He is honest and lives above reproach in both his personal life and in ministry.

In working with sponsors, district officials and the community, Pastor and Sis. Erma Judd, who also encourage and lead me on a daily basis, have taught me abundantly, above, and beyond. They have polished the corners of my life by their exemplary living. They both have demanding schedules, but I can't think of a time when our family was in need that they didn't drop everything for us. They have done this for countless others as well. In business, they operate honestly and on a level most would not. If you hand them a five-dollar bill for the ministry, that gift gets entered as an offering, even if it means turning it in two weeks later when they return home; it is not their cup of Starbucks while working on company time. Now, that might sound to some like a small thing to share, but is it really? I have served for over twenty-five years now as the Director of Sponsor

Relations. My department has been trusted with millions of dollars throughout that time. I am thankful for mentors like the Judds, who have modeled the importance of accountability when it comes to God's money. Not only through tithing, but also in making sure that our donors' dollars are spent as they have expected. Through this level of Christian integrity, God's blessings can be poured out.

Bro. and Sis. Judd have also guided me as I have sought out other businesses, giving me sound wisdom and direction. I'm an overachiever who wants to conquer the world, but they have taught me to keep first things first. This lesson in prioritizing has proven successful in my life. Whether as my boss, my pastor, or my friends, the Judds are there for me. Their leadership is one I hold in high esteem. Not only do they have a wealth of knowledge to share, but they also listen to their staff and allow us to cast our own vision. I still have a voice. Please understand, when you allow a man of God and his wife to lead, guide, instruct, and mentor you, it does not mean you will always love everything they have to say. When you do this, you are giving them permission to help you see things differently, correct, and admonish when necessary. I have spoken to Sis. Judd often, especially in the early years of marriage. I have unloaded onto her about my husband in hopes that she would jump to my defense and wholeheartedly agree with me. That seldom happened. Instead, she taught me truths I needed to learn, truths about myself, and a better approach to handling matters. Sis. Judd comes from a childhood more similar to mine; seeing her walk in dignity and grace, never allowing her past to dictate her future, has served me well. She is the **Proverbs 31** lady if ever I have known one.

Ken Burton, who was my boss for over twenty years, was also a mentor in my life. I have met with him hundreds of times over the years. He can turn a dime into a dollar. He has the golden touch and operates at the highest level of integrity and Christian example. He has transferred a wealth of knowledge to me, so much so that this book could not have been written without the abundant amount of information I have learned from him. I have seen Bro. Burton face many trials with dignity and grace. I have watched him put out fires so thoroughly you never even knew there was a flame. He is the kindest, most graceful person you could know, and is always positive, believing only the best in all mankind. My love for him and Sis. Margo Burton ranks high. They are among the top ten people in my book.

Deanna Knight is another business mentor who taught me everything I know about photography. She saw potential in me when I was in my early twenties. Even though she never had anything to gain, she has always taught me well, and I treasure the expertise she passed on to me.

More recently, I have found a mentor in Michelle Pace, who serves on our cabinet as our Executive Assistant to the President. I tease Michelle often, telling her that God sent her to Tupelo Children's Mansion to teach me more of what I need to know. Michelle is a prayer warrior. She fasts often, loves unconditionally, and loves Bible  Quizzing. Michelle has written two books, and it was through reading her story, that I found the courage to write mine.

Through the entire process of writing this, she has walked beside me, encouraging me to tell my story openly and honestly while showing me the mechanics along the way.

We need mentors in our lives. We need people to help us grow and become the best versions of ourselves. If you don't have a mentor because you think you know it all, don't expect to get very far in life. Do not be an island unto yourself. Grow yourself, and grow others.

A best friend is someone who understands your past, believes in your future, and accepts you for the way you are today.
Unknown

Building a Team

Everybody needs to be running the race with others. No one is safe running alone. Those years of track and cross-country taught me about the power found in numbers and the need for a team. This is no less true when running the race of life. There is something comforting and supportive about having others to rally around you when you can't go on alone. Sometimes, your team may have to drag you across the finish line.

Your team is different from mentors and can include mentors, friends, family, employers, co-workers, or religious leaders. My team is a combination of those who mentor me and those who I mentor. Many times I have needed not only those who have run ahead, but also those who have run alongside me, and even sometimes those who are a few steps behind me.

One of my team members has been Cori Taylor. About the time of my daughter Alayna's birth, Cori's daughter Ava was also being born. Cori was ten years younger than me, and I had mostly served as one of her mentors. She was mature for her age, loved entertaining, and enjoyed doing many of the same things I also enjoyed. Together, we prepared recipes, baked, cooked, planned events, and enjoyed raising our children. I knew her well since I was babysitting her and Shaina when their parents, Tom and Debbie traveled for the Mansion. Our children were raised together, playing soccer,

 swimming, and taking ballet. Camp meetings, cookouts and trips to the mall are among many of our memories together. Cori and I have turned simple birthday parties into massive

events, as people came to celebrate our children. Others came to see what in the world we had planned for the party. We organized Easter, Fall and Christmas parties, requiring our friends to buy matching, monogrammed clothing for their children. I'll never forget the time we threw an Easter party, moving from event to event when I said, "Okay, you kids can take a break and play. Pictures are over." Cori and I burst into laughter. How crazy we were! As I've aged, I realize how silly we must have seemed, but we loved every minute of the adventures. To this day, we still  hold a yearly tradition of a Christmas party for our children. We have experienced the highs of adventures together and the lows of loss, including that of our friend, Harlon.

Many times I have been blessed to pour into Cori's life, but there have also been times when she has strengthened me. Don't think because someone is younger that they can't make a difference in your life. I will never forget the winter day that we sat together in my office and she said, "Annette, you work too much. Look at your kids. They are small, but growing up so fast. You need to slow down."

Those words were not easy to hear, but she was right. I was a "Yes" person. I worked entirely too much and had my hands involved in too many things. After our conversation, I spent the next several days in prayer and made some major changes in my life. I was working full-time at the Mansion, and I changed my hours, cutting down my work days to three per week. I was doing very well with my Scentsy business, but I had no boundaries. I was too available, so I set up a schedule of when I would work and when I would put work aside, completely focusing on playing with my children and being fully present. I was running ragged and missing milestones. Thankfully, a member of my team stepped in and changed my course.

Cori, along with Natania and other friends, such as Annette George, who serves as my Assistant at the Mansion, have been vital members of my team. Annette works under my direction, yet she is almost twenty years my senior. Therefore, she possesses a  wealth of knowledge and has years of experience in a variety of circumstances and situations I have yet to face. In many cases, Annette has been a key player on my team, helping me to cope with life's trials or better understand situations that have come my way. Your "team" may come from various sources.

Some of my key team players have been the leadership at the Mansion with whom I work daily. Melvin and Linda Raab are much older and have been team players who have guided my family by offering wisdom, knowledge, direction, and love. Jennifer Lawrence, who serves as our Director of Education, has been a team leader in my children's lives, and a friend to Robert and me when we have needed advice about their education. Jennifer's two children have always been like family to us. Drew is a mentor to Landon, while our oldest daughter, Teresa, has been a mentor to Ariel. We are all running the race of life at different paces, but we are together, and that brings us all strength. Kathryn and Vance Slagle are also on our team. Kathryn serves as the Director of Residential

Services, and Vance has coached Bible Quizzing intermittently with my husband and me. Our families have traveled the country together. Our friends Larry and Jenny have been a part of our lives since before we married. We have each other's backs. We fight for one another. We help each other. We have all weathered many storms together!

Everyone will not always serve as your mentor. I chose a few mentors and stayed close to those particular people. However, everyone who runs the race beside you, in front of you, and even behind you has something to teach you. We need one another. To cross that finish line into glory, we need others beside us, strengthening us, pulling us along when we are weak, and picking up our baton when we drop it. Even my own adult daughter and her wonderful husband, Brannon, have been important members of my team. They have been there for us in the raising of our children, teaching us by the way they live their lives. I can't even begin to describe how proud I am of their beautiful family, how well they are doing as a young married couple and as parents.

I have been blessed to lead an incredible group of people through my Scentsy home-business team. In some instances, I have taught them. At other times, they have taught me. Someone does not have to be ahead of you in the race for you to grab onto them for a sprint or the long distance journey. What we have accomplished in my Scentsy business has not always been easy. Staying the course has often been difficult. At times, when I have wanted to quit, mentors in my life, such as Krystal Riddle, Debbie Pitts Palmer, and Allison Dalke, are the ones who kept me going when I did not have the strength to stand. Those ladies are all one level ahead of me, at the top of our company, and I was blessed to look up to them when I could not find my own way. It is about helping others and allowing them to help you. If we don't do this, we can become very discouraged and fall away. I once heard it said that people go where they are invited, but they stay where they feel they belong. Join a group which gives you a sense of belonging, and stick with them. And, when the going gets tough, latch on! I have too many Scentsy team members to begin naming them. They are not a number. They are people, real people like me. I count it an honor to have them on my team. I make it my mission to speak into their lives, but so many times, they have spoken into mine. We are a family. Just recently, one of our team members was going through the trial of her life. She reached her team numbers, but she wasn't going to achieve her personal retail numbers, which would have affected her bonus. Not on our watch! Everyone started placing orders from her website. When she felt like all hope was lost, her team joined arms and let her know we cared.

My best friend in high school was Karen Zimay. She and I ran the two-mile race together. We kept each other steady and strong, helping each other take the next step. We were competitive, but only in the way that pushed us both to be the best versions of ourselves. We did not gloat or flaunt the times we beat each other in the race. We were partners, and we had each other's back. Getting to that finish line often only happened because she was just ahead, pulling me forward.

Life is demanding, and no matter how much you do to live to the best of your ability, trials come. Sometimes, trials vacation for just a little while, and in other instances, they move in like new tenants. Fight through these times with a team. Rely on others. Reach out. Pray and fast; it is necessary. Reading the Word is a must. Everyone needs a team of people to rally around them when life gets tough. My team has proven themselves. They have carried me when I could not take another step. My team has run beside me when the way seemed dark, and it wasn't easy to find the light. They have helped carry our family through trials when we could not see through the pain. They have helped light our path. You need friends. You need a team!

Plugging into the Light Source

Every wise woman buildeth her house: but the foolish plucketh it down with her hands.
Proverbs 14:1

The key to bringing light to our world is plugging into our light source. We must look to our Lord and Savior, Jesus Christ, the light of the World, for our *daily* strength! That does not mean pray only during times of *crisis*. It means we have to fill our cup.

When I got saved, Brother and Sister Watts bought me my first Bible. It was beautiful, and I read it through and through. I marked favorite and helpful passages of scripture. Though it is too worn to even use now, it is a treasured possession, a trophy. That little country church did not just invite me; they taught me to "Read the Word!" We must be plugged into His precepts more than being plugged into social media or the news.

Did you know that we can talk to our Savior about our *needs, wants, aspirations, fears,* and *doubts*? God can do more for us in sixty seconds, than our friends, pastors, or co-workers can do in sixty minutes!

Those happy people in that little Pentecostal church taught me this scripture.

Be careful for nothing; but in every thing by prayer and supplication with thanksgiving let your requests be made known unto God. And the peace of God, which passeth all understanding, shall keep your hearts and minds through Jesus.
Philippians 4:6-7

When the Light Goes Out

Maybe you're reading this book and you feel like you have no light. Could it be that the circumstances of life have robbed you of joy? Maybe you're still single and asking yourself why? You might think you're an emotional mess, coping with feelings of rejection, wondering why God just will not give you what you want. You long to be loved, but feel unlovable.

Maybe you have suffered a tragic divorce that left you broken and alone. Maybe you're married but are experiencing great pain that nobody else perceives. You smile, carry out your responsibilities and duties, work, pray, take care of your home, and conduct yourself with a "business as usual" attitude. It takes everything you have just to put one foot in front of the other. If the truth be told, you are merely existing. These feelings of pain and despair are real and raw, but you think you have no one on whom you can lean. Oh, my friend, but you do. You have Jesus, and you have the saints of the most-high God. Please reach out and make others aware. Please know that He cares, and so do His people.

Maybe you're a newlywed and your Prince Charming, isn't quite as charming as he was in the beginning of your relationship. Could it be that secret sins have surfaced and you feel like what should have been a fairytale feels more like a nightmare? Oh sweet friend, I want you to know, there is hope. Others have walked your path. Others, even those in ministry, have felt your pain. You are not alone. There is help, and there is hope. Don't go by yourself. Reach out!

Maybe you're a parent who carries a heavy heart. You are trying to live for God and raise your children in a Godly home, but in your eyes, your spouse isn't doing his part, and you feel you're single-handedly fighting the fight. Maybe he attends church with you, but he does not live for God as passionately as you feel he should. If so, let me tell you that there is hope! There is always hope.

Maybe you're just simply exhausted. Being a mama of a little one...or two...or three...or more...is work. You feel drained with a house that never stays clean. When one baby stops crying, another is making a mess! It feels like a never-ending rat race, and you're always comparing yourself to your friend Suzy on Instagram, who makes every gluten-free, sugar-free, soy-free meal from scratch. She is quick to show the cyber world her beautifully-dressed children, who are perfect in every possible way.

Maybe for you, your nest is now empty, and you still can't believe the time with your children is gone. Some years may have been more strenuous than others, but you never expected the time to end. You miss the mess. The muddy shoes and backpacks filled with candy wrappers and last month's study guides are crumbled and gone. What happened? Where did two decades go? They are now grown and independently making their own choices without your hand to continuously hold. Maybe you don't always like their choices; your inability to have that same influence you once had, is incomprehensible to you. These are natural, normal feelings that most parents experience. You will get through this difficult season.

Maybe you are serving in full-time ministry, but you have suffered deep wounds in the church. You've been misunderstood or feel taken for granted. Hurt. Offended. Beaten down. Oh friend of mine, we all have felt something of that nature sometime or another, just as Paul did on his journeys. Saving lives is not for the faint of heart. Changing eternity is not a walk in the park. But keep walking! If you don't have the strength to walk, crawl. If you can't crawl, sit still. Hope and help are available. Please call a friend, a mentor, or your pastor. Allow yourself to be weak, so others can help give you strength. I can't tell you how many times I have needed the unity of the body of Christ to help pull my family out of crisis. Yes, there is sometimes, pain, heartache, and sickness, *in* the church. After all, the church is our hospital, so stay there when you're sick or injured. Don't run away from Doctor Jesus and His assistants who have come in the form of saints to help nurse you back to spiritual health.

The truth is, there is always a valley at the bottom of a mountain. Sometimes the visit to the valley feels much too long, and you feel unequipped for the climb to the top. You're able to make the trek, even if you need a helping hand to pull you *up* along the way. If you need that helping hand, it is okay. It is never a sign of weakness to need strength. You are not a failure if you have failed. All hope is not lost. It may feel like it at the moment, but it is not. You may need to go through this rough season to come out more refined from the fire. You may need to find your path through the practice of fasting.

Sometimes our light goes out but is blown again into instant flame by an encounter with another human being.
Albert Schweitzer

Pushing Away from the Table

The saints loved to pray both at Bible College and in the "Happy People's" church! We would stay up all night praying! I will never forget the time my youth pastor's wife, Martha, and I got so excited over the new pews the church had received, that we decided to have an all-day prayer meeting. We anointed the pews with oil. That was an amazing, spiritual afternoon until we got overzealous and accidently spilled our oil all over one of the new benches! What can I say? We were on fire!

Although the Happy People loved McDonald's, they also practiced fasting! They taught us to push away from the table. They told me I needed to *hunger* for *God* more than I hungered for the things of this world. *I promise you this*, if you make fasting your practice, your life can and *will* change. Years after I married, I was in a low spot in life. I was exhausted, overweight, and needed some miracles in my life. I called my friend Terri, and she asked me to meet her at a gas station about fifteen minutes away. This was half-way between our two houses. It was late, but she could feel my pain and desperation through the phone. I pulled up to the station, and she immediately got out of the car. She came over and sat in my passenger seat. She looked me in the eyes and asked, "Annette, are you fasting?" Well, no, I wasn't. She gave me a book and urged me to begin a fast. She shared many stories with me on fasting and reminded me that the only way my circumstances might truly change would be through a fast. I went home and read the entire book. I did not sleep. I devoured every word. I drank in each chapter. I was hungry for change. Through my reading, I realized that I needed that spiritual hunger to change me. That hunger for change would

result in pushing away from what I loved most... *Food.*
Somewhere along the way, food had become my answer to far
too many problems. Instead of craving more of God and
seeking His face, I found refuge in the refrigerator. That night
I began a seven-day fast. I did not touch food for the next
week. I drank water, and I fell on my face crying out to the
Lord for His mercy, His love, His direction, and His wisdom.

*Therefore also now, saith the Lord, turn ye even to me with all your
heart, and with fasting, and with weeping, and with mourning.*
Joel 2:12

Through that fast came deliverance from myself! Chains were
broken. Deliverance from sugar came. Worries and fears
subsided. True joy returned. I found peace that passed all
understanding. I found my fire for God again. I fell back in
love with my Savior! I had new purpose.

If you find yourself in a dry and barren land, push away from
the table. It will initiate a thirst for God like you have never
known. When we completely empty ourselves, there is room
for Him to fill us to overflowing. If you're hurting, go on a
fast. If you feel lost, push away from food. If you're fearful,
find refuge in feeding on the Word of God and empty your
reliance on the temporal, like food. If you have been hurt by a
spouse, friend, boss, pastor or someone who is considered a
leader in your life, go on a fast. Nothing can cleanse our souls
like fasting can. That seven-day fast has led me to many more
since, including one that was fourteen days and simply life-
changing.

I now try to do at least a few longer fasts a year as well as
several one to two day fasts per week. This keeps me on
course. If I don't fast and pray for my children, who will? If I
don't fight for my family, my marriage, my husband, who

will? I am called by God and so are you! Never give up. We must be relentless in our pursuit. Remember that fasting must be coupled with prayer.

When God calls me to a lengthy fast, I used to think it was unspiritual to tell my children, but it is not. They need to learn that some things in life can only come to pass through this form of consecration. In recent years, we have called a few family fasts. We did not put any certain requirements upon the kids pertaining to food, but we did ask them to give up something of their own choice. We have done a month-long media fast, and it brought a closeness into our home that had been missing for a while.

So we fasted and besought our God for this: and he was intreated of us." **Ezra 8:23**

Seek ye First His Kingdom

*Seek ye first, the kingdom of God, and his righteousness; and all
these things shall be added unto you."*
Matthew 6:33

To the person who longs to marry, fall so deeply in love with
Christ that you don't feel the pressure to take a selfie a day,
positioned just perfectly, to prove your worth. Work to keep
yourself pure and righteous in His sight, and He will meet
your needs. Understand that no one can give you the security
that God can. Only God can meet your deepest desires. Fall in
love with His Word because the more you read it, the more
you will hunger for it!

To the newlywed whose love has already begun to lack a little
luster, I urge you to stop living in a fairytale. No one but Jesus
can truly satisfy your deepest longings. I too was once a
newlywed. The first time I discovered that my prince wasn't
always as charming as I first thought he was, my dreams of
utopia came crashing down. The best book I read as a young
bride was called *Love and Respect*. Purchase that book, and
read it until you can't do anything else but be respectful! You
can have a full, happy, Godly marriage, but you may have to
stop being critical and demanding. Get out of the romance
novels and into the book that will breathe life into your soul
and marriage.

I have now been married a few decades. I love my marriage,
and I am grateful for my husband. He is not perfect, but no
man is perfect. I feel safer and stronger with him by my side.
He is not my be-all and end-all. He is not my safety net, my
security blanket, or my lifeline. God is! Yes, I love my
husband. Yes, I need my husband. I treasure this man God

gave me, but when times are tough, and it feels like the world all around me is crashing, I find my true refuge in God. I find my peace through prayer, answers when I fast, hope and joy when I worship my Maker. No one can give you the peace that God can. When we expect people to constantly give us peace and joy, we become disappointed and disillusioned. Only God can truly heal the deep pains of our heart and provide clarity in times of chaos. Give safety when we feel afraid. Stop the raging storm when we feel trapped. God wants to be our answer to every need. He longs for us to fill our lives with His presence. Get in His Word. If you don't hear Him speaking to you through the pages of the Bible, read on. Read His love letter to you until your eyes hurt and you just can't focus another minute. Get into Psalms and Proverbs. Find power through praise! Read and read and read some more, and in time, the clanging and clatter of this world will mean little to you. Why? Because God can and will breathe life into you through His Word.

Forgiveness

If you're alive, you have been hurt. Forgiveness is part of God's remedy for receiving healing. Maybe you're longing to forgive but also need help in the process. This may very well be the chapter you wish was not in the book. If you have been hurt by your parents, your siblings, a friend, a leader, a co-worker, a saint, or even a stranger, it is my goal that you can learn to lay your hurt aside. By doing so, you will unlock blessings in your life.

And when ye stand praying, forgive, if ye have ought against any: that your Father also which is in heaven may forgive you your trespasses.
Mark 11:25

As you have read my story, you may be wondering how I chose the path of forgiveness. Many people who have a story like mine, use it for a crutch the rest of their lives. Unfortunately, it happens far too often. This grieves me. When the Bible speaks of forgiveness, it repeatedly admonishes us to forgive others of their trespasses, just as He has forgiven us of ours. I realize that this isn't always easy. We are not instructed to forget. We are urged to forgive. These are two entirely different things.

I have forgiven every person who has hurt me, whether it was sexual molestation, rape, cruel words or deeds, taking advantage, using me, or betrayal. I forgave for me, not for them! We can't always control the pain that others cause or inflict. However, we choose not to pass sentence on ourselves, only to be locked in the prison of pain forever. Forgiveness does not give us amnesia. We will still remember how it felt to be hurt. We will carry scars. In some ways, our pain will shape our direction on the road of life, but we choose how we stay the course in response to hurt.

> *And forgive us our debts, as we forgive our debtors.*
> **Matthew 6:12**

When we pray this prayer, we need to think about what this verse means. When we release forgiveness, we allow God to forgive us! If you are living in pain, ask God to search your heart. Are you harboring bitterness because you cannot forgive? Is the deep suffering of yesterday your place of safety today? Does it comfort you? Does it make you feel justified in your pain? Could it be that you're hosting a pity party for yourself? Are you justifying sin or mistakes in your own life because of a significant painful event that occurred in your past?

> *And be ye kind one to another, tenderhearted, forgiving one another, even as God for Christ's sake hath forgiven you.*
> **Ephesians 4:32**

Although we are required to forgive, we can take comfort in knowing that God takes care of the details regarding those who have hurt us. Romans 12:20 says:

> *Dearly beloved, avenge not yourselves but rather*
> *give place unto wrath: for it is written,*
> *Vengeance is mine; I will repay, saith the Lord.*
> *Therefore if thine enemy hunger, feed him;*
> *if he thirst, give him drink:*
> *for in so doing thou shalt heap coals of fire on his head.*

That is harsh. We are commanded *not* to take vengeance. It is *not* our place to *get even*. We are actually told to do the opposite, that is, be kind. God has this.

If you want to heal your hurts, ask the Lord right now to help you forgive. He can heal your heart. In some instances, as we are told in the Word, you can take your hurt before your brother or sister in Christ. However, our efforts may not be received in the way we had hoped.

I shared my heart with my father. I told him the pain he had caused. With tears streaming down my cheeks, I bared my soul. He cried too. As he wept, I knew he was broken, and I instantly handed him grace. Even though my pain was still there, his heart was sincere, and I could not withhold my forgiveness toward him.

With my mom, forgiveness wasn't as simple. I wrote my Mother a letter when I was in Bible School. I shared my hurts. I asked questions, but it did not go the way I had hoped. She was enraged and took no responsibility or ownership for anything I mentioned. Mom came to know God, yet she also never fully apologized to me. I had to come to terms with that. I had to love her and offer forgiveness despite her denial. She needed God, and I was a living testimony to His grace. If I would have never forgiven her, I'm not sure what the outcome would have been in her life. Most importantly, I know that mine would look very differently.

We cannot live with people without experiencing pain. In our lifetimes, we will, unfortunately, be the people who sometimes cause hurt to others. Even your most well intentioned saints are going to cause hurt, confusion, division or discomfort at some point in their lives. We are not perfect people. If we were, I would never have needed to write this book.

Forgive others. Forgive yourself. It will inevitably free you to live fully and completely. It will empower you to walk in

newness of life. Forgiveness will equip you to change others'
lives. Get outside of yourself, and let God have His way!

To win the fight, you've got to have the right strategy and the
right resources because victories don't come by accident.
From the War Room

Time, Talent, and Treasure

Giving of our tithes and offerings is Biblical. It is sound doctrine. It is *not* a question concerning whether or not we have the money. We give because it belongs to God. From the time I was a small child, I found joy in giving. I gave away my lunch. I gave away my snack funds. I shared with anyone. As a young person, I would give all I had, even foolishly sometimes. However, there was never a single time I can remember that God did not supply my needs.

If you don't have much money, give your time. This was also something I practiced as a child, curiously enough, having learned it from my parents. They clearly had their faults, but I have learned in my life that some of the most hardened people, still also give! In an effort to relieve my mind from thoughts of my present suffering, I would help someone else whose situation seemed worse than mine. If you want to get over yourself, stop looking in the mirror. Stop taking selfies. Right now, I want you to put the book down and consider your surroundings.

What is happening in your home? Do your children need help with their homework? Is your spouse stressed after a long day? Does the elderly neighbor across the street need help with his yard-work? Is a friend at work or church hurting? Do you know a single mom of three who has not had a break in months? What about the handicapped? The homeless? The friend whose marriage is falling apart? The father of a child who battles addiction? The misunderstood family whose little boy was diagnosed with autism? What about the slacker? The person who can't ever seem to rise above their circumstances? Maybe they don't know how to ask for help. Maybe they need a friend or a mentor! People need people.

Lastly, but certainly not least, we can give our talent! In the process of writing this book, God sent me an editor! I'd been praying. I'd been fasting. I said, "God, please send me the right person to edit my book. Someone who can literally stop their life to finish this manuscript." As He always does, God came through in the way of Cindy Moore! Not only did I find one excellent editor, but I was also blessed with her editing mentor, Pam Eddings. Now "I" have new mentors and new friends. God works that way you know!

Ask yourself, what talents am I hiding? Maybe you don't have a lot of money to give, but do you have sound advice about finances? Would that knowledge help someone else get out of debt? There is talent inside of you. Don't hide it. Share it! One act of kindness could have a massive effect, changing not only one person's life but also thousands!

...freely ye have received, freely give.
Matthew 10:8

Believing in His Promises

...as for me and my house, we will serve the LORD!
Joshua 24:15

To the one who is living with an unsaved spouse, hang onto this scripture and declare it. Pray it. Claim it. Believe God for it! Love your husband as if he is doing everything right. Don't be a martyr or a nagger. Build him up...and stay true to God. Let His light shine through you. My friend Michelle Pace wrote an incredible book entitled, *A Legacy of Grace.* She lived with an unsaved spouse for twenty-six years, and it wasn't easy. She describes a scene in the book where she had just decorated for Christmas when he came home and ransacked the house in a fit of rage. After two and a half decades, she won her husband to Christ. Today, her three adult girls are living in the truth! Was it easy? NO! She fought Hell for his salvation only to end up losing him two years later to cancer. Michelle never gave up praying for her husband, and one day she will walk with him on streets of gold.

Sometimes it may seem like the battle is too long. The fight is too tough. The situation may look impossible.

But Jesus beheld them, and said unto them, With men this is impossible; but with God all things are possible.
Matthew 19:26

There is nothing God cannot do! I have seen Him perform many miracles. I may not know what your need is, but He does! Everyone in your circle does not have to know your needs. God is enough. This is something that causes many people to struggle. We have needs, hurts, and struggles. We think the only way our needs can be met or fulfilled is to tell the world, or at least our top five friends. While at times it is helpful to confide in a trusted friend, just know that no one can meet or satisfy your needs like Jesus can. No one can heal your hurting heart like He can. No one can satisfy your longing soul like He can. Your closest friends can sympathize or even empathize with you, and maybe even give sound advice, but God can also perform a miracle at just the mention of His name. He knows our hearts and our needs before we even ask Him.

Rely on scripture. When you're in a low place in your life, fall in love with the Word of God. As I write this book, my husband and I are *listening* to scripture for at least thirty minutes a day. It has served as a powerful tool for us during what feels like a trying season. My husband bought us the *Words of Promise Audio Bible*, and it has spoken into our hearts and minds as we listened. It is amazing how much we have fallen in love with stories we have heard for years, finding a multitude of joy, peace, and direction from the lives of Abraham, Isaac, Jacob, and Joseph. As we listen to their struggles, though they occurred ages ago, it is amazing how relatable these Biblical events become when you're in need of answers. When your struggles become bigger than every day time-management, addressing the needs of the kids, and getting the bills paid, seek God. When you need real answers, they can be found in the Word of God. We have been drawn deeply into its truths. After listening each night, my husband does research and expounds a little more on what we just heard. Each night in our home, we have always had family devotions or at least a time of prayer with our children. However, we have not studied the Word like we should. This new scriptural discourse has brought greater depth to our marriage, and has helped us navigate our way through deeper waters. There is so much power in the Word!

Miracles

I spoke in an earlier chapter about my friend Janice being healed. Next to my personal salvation experience, that was the first physical miracle I had encountered. Not long after, my nephew, Jason, broke his ankle and was rushed to the emergency room. The doctor ordered x-rays and told us that Jason's ankle was fractured and possibly broken. Placing a temporary cast on it, they gave him crutches and made him an appointment to meet with the orthopedic doctor on Monday. I love all three of my nephews, and Brandon and Ryan hold a special place in my heart. However, Jason has always been the closest to me, and he was the one I spoiled the most. I did not want my little buddy to suffer. He adored his auntie and believed pretty much anything I told him, so off to church we went. I took Jason into the church and sat him on the altar. I read him a scripture on healing and told him that all we had to do was believe and pray, and God could do the rest. He said, "I believe Aunt Sam!"

Jason's faith was all God needed. We prayed a simple prayer, and Jason leaped up from the altar! He left his crutches up front and began to run around the church! I freaked out! "Jason," I said, "Are you okay?"

He replied, "Yes, Aunt Sam; God has healed me!" I brought Jason home from church without a limp or crutches. Mom and my sister could not believe all that we shared. Wendy took Jason to the surgeon the next morning as she had been instructed to do. She knew Jason felt better, but she also needed a doctor's opinion. She was astonished when the surgeon said he could not see any fracture at all. His original x-rays showed a clear fracture. The doctor was stunned! He thought he must have been sent the wrong x-rays. Being perplexed, the doctor decided to x-ray both ankles. It did not make sense. There was no sign of trauma! Jason left the doctor's office with a confirmation of the healing God had performed for him the previous night. This experience left a deep impression on my sister. She and I have discussed it many times over the years. Another seed of faith was planted in my mother's heart. There was no denying that Jesus had His hand on Jason.

I told the story about Marie who was instantly healed at Walgreen's. Her healing was a physical miracle that took place right before my eyes. However, that was only one of many miracles God performed in that store. I quickly became an evangelist to quite a few people. They shared their lives with me. I prayed for everything, including physical ailments, financial needs, and family issues.

One day a customer came into the store, and as he walked past me, he turned around and said, "You must be a Christian because Jesus is all around you. I wasn't feeling God a minute ago, but I felt Him instantly as I walked past you." The only explanation I have is that I lived in prayer and the Word, fasting often, and my faith stayed strong.

Financial miracles have taken place for me since the day I gave my life to God. Every dollar I ever needed during my years at Bible College was provided. Throughout that time, I worked hard and learned good stewardship. I paid every penny toward my bill. However, my earnings were never enough. Every week, without any prompting from me, people gave me money. I could not leave church without Pastor Urshan or someone else placing a $20 bill in my hand. It was amazing, and I just praised God every time. On a trip to the *Because of the Times* conference, only one month after arriving at Bible College, a man walked up to me and said he admired my worship, and God had told him to give me some money. He handed me a $100 bill and asked for my name and address. For the next four years, that dear saint sent me the entire set of *Because of the Times* sermons on tape. He never forgot me, and I have listened to those messages over and over, for years.

I mentioned that I arrived at Bible College with very little. No pictures for the walls. No pretty decorations for the room. Nothing. I guess it must have bothered my teachers, though it honestly mattered very little to me. During a Thanksgiving break, Sis. Vickers and Sis. Dugas decided to take matters into their own hands. They decorated my room with gorgeous bedding, beautiful lace curtains, pictures, and rugs. It was incredible. I left an empty space and returned to a dream room. From that moment on, my room was showcased when prospective students came to tour the campus. God provides. He cares about even the smallest details of our lives. I graduated from college having received an Associate's Degree in Theology and a Bachelor's Degree in Christian Education, without an ounce of debt. When I left for my new mission field, I had no money to take with me, but my dear friends, David and Wes, used their car and gas to drive me from Bible College to Tupelo Children's Mansion. I arrived with virtually nothing, yet in no time at all, a bed and a dresser were offered to me by staff members. Bro. Burton taught me how to save and budget my money, later helping me to purchase brand new furniture, pictures, and a car.

During our marriage, God has blessed us so many times we have lost count. Checks have arrived in the mail out of thin air. Blessings were sent by friends who had heard from God. Pay-raises came right as we prayed specifically for certain things we needed. Just yesterday, my dear friend Summer

McChristian, tremendously blessed my life. She said she did it because God told her to do so. Summer and I met just a few years ago, and God has allowed her to be instrumental in my life, and allowed me to also minister to her. God gifts us with massive blessings like this. At times, when we have wanted to take the children out of town, He has afforded us this opportunity in the most unlikely ways. When we wanted to purchase our first home, He provided the means for the down-payment in weeks. We worked for it, but God placed opportunities in our path and gave us direction on how to walk the road and make it work. Those are miracles!

When my son Landon was very young, his hands were covered in warts. My husband put every kind of medicine imaginable on his hands, hoping to heal them. The warts were not hurting him, but he was chewing them off and causing his fingers to bleed. I went on a fast. Three days into it, Landon woke up with every single wart gone. They had fallen off in his bed. Only God can do these things!

A few years ago, I received a call from a local friend in Tupelo. She worked at a place called Doctors and Nurses. She said, "Annette, we need you to come here. We have a client who needs prayers." I had no idea what the situation was.

When I arrived, I was taken to a lady in a wheel chair. Her legs and feet were covered in layers of bleeding eczema. The layers on her feet were about two inches thick. I knelt down beside her and asked her if she knew that Jesus loved her and could heal her. She said, "Yes." This lady was obviously in dire need and living in pain. I prayed, "Lord, your Word says you are a healer, and we need a miracle today. Please help my new friend, and give her brand new feet."

It makes no sense why I was surprised. The next morning my friend called me. "Annette, God healed her! Her feet and legs are completely healed. It is as if they are brand new." Only God can do these things!

For a season of time at the Mansion, God placed some very dear friends in our lives. They had been trying to have children for many years. Angela was serving as my assistant at the time. It was difficult to see her suffering due to her longing for a baby. She and I had been praying about this matter and decided to go on a fast. During the time, I was randomly asked to take calls for the front office. I had never worked there, but I agreed to go that morning. A call was received from a young lady who was pregnant and due to deliver any day. She had just read the Mansion Tidings and wanted to speak to our editor who just happened to be me. I asked her how I could help.

She said, "Well, I know you're going to think this is crazy, but I'm having a baby in a few days, and God told me to give him to Tupelo Children's Mansion. I have picked out a couple who I would like to parent my son. He is the man who wrote the back page article in your recent magazine."

I could not believe my ears. What was happening? Was I even allowed to have this conversation? Was this possible? Like Esther, God puts us in the right place at the right time. Within days, this young girl was in Tupelo, placing her son into the arms of my dear friends. She has never once looked back or harassed them in any way. It was a rare miracle, and I was honored to play a small role in watching God do His work. I was blessed to be with the Parkers during this entire process and still count them as close friends.

Other miracles I have witnessed have occurred when families were in crisis. I have seen God put marriages back together. I have seen children completely delivered from drugs. I have been used to provide financial miracles for others at times when God has asked us to give. Our God is a miracle-working God! There is nothing He cannot do. All He asks is that we have faith. We pray. We believe. He does the work. When the miracles don't come when we want, we have to trust Him and His perfect timing.

And he was teaching in one of the synagogues on the sabbath. And, behold, there was a woman which had a spirit of infirmity eighteen years, and was bowed together, and could in no wise lift up herself. And when Jesus saw her, he called her to him, and said unto her, Woman, thou art loosed from thine infirmity. And he laid his hands on her: and immediately she was made straight, and glorified God.
Luke 13:10-13

In Bible College, my close friend Robyn, was very shy. She felt called to ministry but lacked boldness. A few years ago, while preaching, her pastor pointed to her and said, "Robyn, there is a demand on your life." Robyn was stirred. She knew God had called her to witness to her boss, Debbie. She answered God's call and won Debbie to the Lord. Since that event occurred, Debbie began witnessing to her family, and as they were saved, they witnessed to their friends, who also witnessed to friends. Nearly 200 people have now visited their church, and 75 of them have been baptized in Jesus' name! Robyn and her husband Jeff, have loved these people and have seen God restore lives and perform so many miracles, it would require writing a separate book. Robyn says that if you make a friend, you make a disciple. There is no miracle too big for our God!

Standing in the Gap

Many of you who are reading this book are tired, even exhausted. You may even be surprised you picked up this book or kept reading this far. Why? You have a plateful of responsibility, and there are only so many hours in a day. So much is at our disposal, and it is easy for even the most consistent, disciplined person not to have *social media attention deficit disorder*. The world is moving at such a fast pace, and nothing holds our attention for long. We are constantly moving, searching, reading, watching, and comparing. But what are we actually accomplishing? That is a question I often ask myself.

If you're a mom, and you're anything like me, you want a clean house. We want to have all the laundry done at one time. We want perfection. Despite the fact that you think your neighbor's house looks perfect, that is not reality. If you still have children at home, take the time to hold them close. When you have to choose between cleaning or praying, pray while you clean; just make sure you pray. Throughout the years, my husband has said many times, "Stop what you're doing and come play a board game with us." Or he would say, "Sit down and play. The house is fine. Our kids won't be little for long." He taught me to rest and enjoy my children. I wish I could take back the many days when I did not take time. So many missed moments. So many lost opportunities. Once our children are grown, we are left with a pile of pictures and a room full of left-behind, dusty trophies. Only one of my children has currently left the nest and is married with children. I miss the days Teresa wanted me to run to the mall with her, or help her make a costume, or the times she would wake us in the middle of the night because she had received a revelation in scripture or heard from the Lord. I did not always treasure each and every moment as I should have.

As important as playing with our kids is, we have to remember that we must PRAY for our children! If we don't stand in the gap for our kids, who will? Our prayers are stored up in heaven. God hears. God sees. We need His strength!

Our children face many temptations and struggles. The schools are filled with unchurched kids, and our children will either influence them or be influenced by them. There is nothing in between. If we are not praying parents, how can they stand a chance? I'm not a prayer warrior, so please do not misunderstand me. I love God with all of my heart, but I'm also just like the next person. Each day is a struggle. My flesh wants to do anything except pray. In all honesty, I want to go to the gym. I want the house sparkling clean. I want to get on social media and see what all of my friends are doing. I don't want to pray! But, we are urged to pray in scripture.

Watch and pray, that ye enter not into temptation: the spirit indeed is willing, but the flesh is weak.
Matthew 26:41

That scripture lets us know that if we don't pray, we ourselves will fall into temptation. How can we fight for our children if we ourselves are not saved? We cannot! Without a daily talk with God, our thoughts become jaded. Without talking to the Savior and listening to His voice, we begin to hear the voices of the world. There is so much commotion happening in the world. Actions once identified as sin are now right in man's eyes. Everything is shifting. Sin wears so many different outfits. If we are not careful, some of those sins become right in our eyes. How does this happen? Slowly. It creeps in like a thief in the night. Day by day, without prayer, we lose our grasp of once closely-kept convictions and find ourselves in unchartered territory. We must pray! Not only for ourselves, but also for our families, our children, our children's children, and our children's friends. I'm honored and privileged to have a few friends who are prayer warriors. I can't tell you how many times I have counted on them to pray. Just knowing that Terri and Michelle were both on their knees for me, gave me the strength to persevere.

We must endure in the war between God and Evil so our children and families don't become lost in the battle. We must claim the words of Deuteronomy so our children will not only live a prosperous life, but also one of promise.

I call heaven and earth to record this day against you, that I have set before you life and death, blessing and cursing: therefore choose life, that both thou and thy seed may live: That thou mayest love the LORD thy God, and that thou mayest obey his voice, and that thou mayest cleave unto him: for he is thy life, and the length of thy days: that thou mayest dwell in the land which the LORD sware unto thy fathers, to Abraham, to Isaac, and to Jacob, to give them.
Deuteronomy 30:19-20

Living the Word

Our children must see us reading the Bible and living by its principles. Enrolling them in a Christian school and keeping them in church every time the doors are open is not enough. We have to teach them to pray, study, and fast.

I was in my late teens before I learned about the self-sacrifices of Ruth, whose friendship and devout loyalty to her mother-in-law is laced throughout that entire book of the Bible. The Hebrew word for Ruth means *friendship* or *companion*. As a parent, it is my calling to teach my children about the power of being a "Ruth" to others.

Before attending a four-year Bible College, I did not know there were lessons to be learned from Delilah. She was a powerful woman who was capable of something an entire Philistine army was not. She was only one woman, but she was also powerful and deceitful enough to bring down Samson, using her beauty and deception. Wow! That is a powerful story. We see it happen every day, in and out of the church. The world is full of Delilah's who seek to destroy men for their own personal gain. If I don't open the Word of God and teach these truths to my children, who will? These stories contain situational truths that we still face today. We must be in the Word and diligent about studying its message. The men and young boys must be warned to guard their minds. As the mother of my household, I must be prayerful and on guard for "Delilah's" who lurk in open spaces or dark places, seeking to destroy. We must learn from these lessons found in the Word of God.

It is our place as parents to teach our children the faithfulness of God that Elizabeth showed, even during times of grave disappointment. We must share the story of Hannah who held onto a dream.

So Hannah rose up after they had eaten in Shiloh, and after they had drunk. Now Eli the priest sat upon a seat by a post of the temple of the LORD. And she was in bitterness of soul, and prayed unto the LORD, and wept sore. And she vowed a vow, and said, O LORD of hosts, if thou wilt indeed look on the affliction of thine handmaid, and remember me, and not forget thine handmaid, but wilt give unto thine handmaid a man child, then I will give him unto the LORD all the days of his life, and there shall no razor come upon his head.

I Samuel 1:9-11

There will be times in our children's lives when they will face great pain, loss, and adversity. Where better to find hope than in the Word? I can't honestly say that my mother ever taught me anything about the Bible. She never once referred to scripture, urged me to read the Word, or told me about the stories of Jesus. However, I did cling to that which she did teach me. She taught me to clean and cook, and she taught me to fight for survival. Until I became a mother myself, I couldn't always see or understand many of the concepts my mother tried to teach me when I was a little girl. This tells me our children are listening to us. They absorb more than we realize, even if they act uninterested in studying the Bible, memorizing scriptures, watching Christian movies or listening to the animated Word through audible. It is still our God-given responsibility to teach them. In fact, it is commanded in the Word that parents teach their children scripture.

And thou shalt teach them diligently unto thy children, and shalt talk of them when thou sittest in thine house, and when thou walkest by the way, and when thou liest down, and when thou risest up.

Deuteronomy 6:7

144

That is powerful! It is our *duty* to instruct our children about the Word of God when they sit in the house, walk through life, lie down to sleep, and wake up in the morning. This passage of scripture gave me pause to consider. We have to rise up as a church! We must be diligent moms and dads. Our children must see the Word of God being read and taught. More importantly, they need to see us model its truths.

Only when it is dark enough can you see the stars.
Martin Luther King Jr.

Painters of Light

We must be careful to remember that we are the *Painter* of *Light* in our homes! We can take what would seem to be the most dismal situation and paint hope, peace, joy, and love into it!

We must choose to build up our families by staying close to Christ, so His light shines through us. We are the ones who cultivate our children's hopes and dreams, and help them to realize that with GOD all things are possible. Because Robert and I were neither one raised in two-parent homes nor taken to church with our mothers, we decided early in our marriage that those things were very important to us. We wanted to raise our children in a happy, Christian home that was full of light, love, and joy, while modeling a peaceful marriage whose cornerstone is Christ Jesus.

As a young couple, we were brimming with optimism and overfilled with positive plans, dreams, ambitions, and hopes for only bright things in our future. We had both known struggles and despair. We had both suffered many disappointments in life, and we talked often of our desire to shield our sweet babies from the harsh realities we had seen and suffered. For the most part, I can honestly say we have accomplished this. Still, like all families, we too have had a few bumps in the road. We have suffered pains, losses and been hurt along the way. And that is okay. If we expect never to experience heartache and disappointment, we are naïve.

My husband lost his best friend in a split second when a drunk driver took his life. This was the most tragic event my children had ever faced. At nine years old, Landon stood beside his best friend, Evan, and helped him pick out his father's coffin. Robert could always count on his friend Harlon. He was that loyal friend who could be trusted and keep your information confidential. He and Robert were college roommates and he had taught Robert how to scuba dive, golf, and even hunt. Our families vacationed together and built our lives one around the other. We celebrated birthday parties and exchanged Christmas gifts. We were lifelong friends. The day Natania called to say that Harlon had been killed shook us to the core. Our little girl Alayna adored him, and Landon looked up to him. When this dark season of life visited us, we had to paint light and life into our home. We could not allow ourselves to sink into depression. These were dark days. We were stunned and shocked. Hurt ran deep, and the questions kept coming, "Why did Uncle Harlon have to die?" In reflection, we referred to God and His Word. It brought hope and peace. We talked of heaven, and how now, more than ever, we wanted to go there so we could one day be reunited with Harlon.

My husband, Robert, has both psoriatic and rheumatoid arthritis as well as severe psoriasis. These medical struggles are real. It is painful to see the amount of medications he is prescribed, and know the levels of pain he suffers. Yet, I seldom hear him say a word. I see his suffering, though I have not always wanted to because it is difficult to admit that he has so many health issues at such a young age. Robert's pain is real and daily present. While he suffers greatly from the pain, he refuses to allow it to immobilize him. We know that God can heal, but we are taught through His Word that it rains on the just and the unjust. Sometimes, people just get sick. Other times people die. The truth of the matter is this, we will all face different and unexpected hurdles, trials, and storms that can't be predicted. During those times, God can usher in unspeakable rest during the unrest. He can bring peace to chaos, and His holy presence can permeate even the most oppressive trials and circumstances. We serve an on-time God, and He is present at just the mention of His name.

My mother was not a believer, but in that tiny tent all those years ago, she reached for me. In that moment of kindness, she helped cultivate a love for people in my twelve-year-old heart. Yes, it is our job to raise our children with Godly admonition, counsel, and correction. After all, we are building future adults. But remember, they also watch our every move, and they catch more of what we do than what we say. Let us love and guide them as Christ would have us do. Sometimes, we will fail, but our number one goal must be to *Live* the *Word!*

Ye are our epistle written in our hearts, known and read of all men.
2 Corinthians 3:2

In a world that feels darker every day, we must find time to spend with God. We are waging a war for our families, and we set the tone in our homes. Even in the bleakest situations, we can choose to show light and instill life, hope, and strength into our children's lives.

Just as a photographer points the reflector into the sun and shines the light onto their subject, we can turn ourselves toward our Lord and Savior and reflect His light to the world. As He shines His light into us, we can shine His light into the lives of others. Each of us has something to offer this world. We can take our own healed brokenness, our times of darkness turned to light, our stories of redemption, and use them to bring the light of Christ to people.

What if those "Happy People" had not decided to shine their light into my life? What if instead, they had chosen to shun or judge me? What if they had not invited me to their little country church? How could they have known that their light shining ever so brightly on me, would one day trickle into the lives of hundreds of children with whom I have been blessed to work at Tupelo Children's Mansion?

You are the Picasso of your palace! Whether it be a tiny apartment, a modest adobe, your dream castle, or a one-room tent, you can choose every day to light the paths of those whose lives you touch.

You can *choose* to plug into the Word, studying it daily. Ask yourself, how much time do you spend reading the Facebook posts of others? Take some of that time and force yourself to read the book of Life. You can choose to get on your knees each day and cry out to God in prayer for your family, for your pastor and pastor's wife, for our nation, and for all whose lives you influence, and who have influence over you. You can choose to push away from the table and find an intimate walk with God through fasting. No, it isn't easy, but turning away from food, denying sweets, or abstaining from whatever we decide, will give us a greater hunger for the Lord and His righteousness. Let us be all that God has called us to be!

Don't ask yourself, "What can others do for me?" Rather, look into the lives of others all around you, and ask yourself, "What can I do for them? How can I bring *value, hope, and light* into their lives?"

About a decade ago, I joined a little candle business called Scentsy. Through this little side business, I have been blessed to make a difference in others' lives, sharing my testimony with people who I would not have otherwise known. It was in my first year of selling when I met Sherry. I could see the look of despair on her face. She was lonely and broken, struggling with some addictions. It did not take a rocket scientist to see her pain. She stopped in my office to bring me some orders, but the truth is, that appointment with me was divinely scheduled by God. I was heading to Oklahoma in just a few days for a Scentsy meeting, and because she seemed to like the product, and I felt like she needed God, I asked her to drive me. Not really knowing me at all, she still went. Sherry's hurts were deep. She did not just have a chip on her shoulder, she carried boulders. She was lugging around heavy weights of shame and pain. She had personal struggles, marriage

 problems, and she was a worried mom, fearful for many reasons and burdened for her boys. Her life was a mess. Thankfully, God is in the business of cleaning up messes. He is a peace speaker, a way-maker. To make a long story short, Sherry not only joined my Scentsy team, but she also joined my church! About six months later, she and her family which included her husband and two sons, followed me to Indianapolis for another Scentsy meeting. While we were there, Bro. Judd was going to be speaking at the Indiana Church Camp Meeting, so we skipped the Scentsy event that the rest of my team was attending and went. Not only were those four filled with the Holy Ghost that night, but their lives were also set to sail an entirely new course. I still talk to Sherry. They have since built a home about an hour away from us and attend another Pentecostal Church, but God still reigns number one in their lives.

We are called to be someone else's light until they can find their own. First and foremost, we must model this at home. We must light our homes with the everlasting light of Christ, so that when the way seems dark, God can be found.

Praise ye the LORD. Blessed is the man that feareth the LORD, that delighteth greatly in his commandments. His seed shall be mighty upon earth: the generation of the upright shall be blessed.
Psalms 112:1

It's for Me, and It's for You

God changed my life at the age of seventeen, and I never once doubted that he could restore my relationship with both of my parents, and restore theirs with me.

During Dad's time in prison, he received what some refer to as jailhouse religion. Mickey Parish from First Baptist Church asked if he could come and talk to Dad about Jesus. He had actually asked Dad several times before; one time, Dad agreed to listen. Mickey had a similar testimony and began to pour out his heart. Dad was impressed by the man's candid nature and openness. He believed him to be sincere. Dad knew he needed God and was tired of living a life of crime. He wanted forgiveness and was told that Jesus could offer that.

By the grace of God, my father surrendered to the Lord. His surrender was on the last day of his prison sentence. Mickey led Dad to the Lord right there in his living room. He had come and witnessed to Dad every week while he served his time. Though Dad was never a "saint" as he would always say, he was no longer the cruel, abusive man Mom once loved. He had stopped working the massive drug rings and calmed down considerably. Once out of prison, he found work, and

began attending church regularly. He also began working in prisons all across the state, leading anyone who would listen to Christ.

I was twenty-one years old when I was reunited with my daddy. He told me about his Pentecostal step-mom who never ceased to pray for him. I will be honest; I did not want to forgive my dad for the awful things he had done. He was a hardened criminal who had drug my mother into the crazy life she led. I fought hard to hold onto bitterness and anger. His story could have been a television crime-thriller. He overcame many obstacles. I am so thankful for our walk on the beach one day so many years ago. Apologies, raw truths, heartfelt hugs - it was real, painful, and revealing. We walked on the sand for what felt like hours. As the waves washed up on the shore, a lifetime of childhood hurts and painful memories began to wash away with the tide. Forgiveness was almost instant. It was a new beginning and a fresh start. A girl never stops needing her daddy, and I happen to believe it is never too late for anyone. I could not hold onto the pain any longer. All that had happened wasn't gone, but it was forgiven. I could clearly see that my dad was now a new man, and our relationship was restored.

Dad told me that his father had married a lady named Bama. She would always have Pentecostal music playing and would preach to my dad. He told her, "Hey, if this Lord you're always talking about is that real, pray me up a wife that will stay with me." He met Miriam the next day and married her thirty-one days later. She stayed with Dad through his many years in prison and stayed with him through the good, the bad, and the pure hell. She loved him, and she fought for what they had.

Our family was driving home from a wonderful week of vacation in Washington DC when the call came. It made no sense to me. I consider myself to be a very strong person, but this call knocked the vacation bliss right out of me. Dad had been sick for a while and in great pain. I had just visited him and spent days beside his hospital bed. He told me he wanted

to fight for more life because he wanted to see my book published. When Miriam awoke that morning, Dad reached for her, and she realized he was fading fast. They were able to hug and say goodbye. She called Hospice.
She called me. While we talked, he drew his last breath. She cried out, "Sam, he's gone! Your dad is gone!" His fight was over. He left this world on July 27th, 2018. It was his final ride. I wept for hours over this call. We had become close and healed the hurt that stood between us, and now he was gone. About an hour after Miriam called, I realized I had a voice mail on my phone. It was from my dad. I couldn't believe it. I listened to it over and over again during our remaining eight-hour drive home. I had tried to call Dad just two days before. I didn't even realize I had missed his return call back to me. He said, "You were thinking about me…and I was thinking about you too. I love you desperately. Please pray for me. It makes no difference what's on the door of the church you go in as long as Jesus resides therein. I love you. I'll talk to you later." We never shared another call, but his message is saved on our computers and phone. His voice remains with me. My friend, Carol, even put his message on a plaque for me. I look at it often.

My step-brother, Adam did a beautiful job handling Dad's memorial service. Though I was never raised with Adam, he was closest to my father because he lived with him longer than any of us. He loved Dad. Adam asked Robert and I to speak at Dad's farewell service. I was nervous. Among family and friends, the place was packed with preachers, police officers and ex-cons. Dad was known and loved by many. I penned this poem and managed to hold back the tears as I read it to honor the life of my father.

His Final Ride

"It's good to see ya Fred," they'd say.
"Well, it's good to be seen," he'd heartily reply.
There was a comfortable easiness about him
That drew you in like a rolling tide.
Dad was first a merchant seaman
Riding the seas wild and keen.
He left the waters and became a chef,
Moving up the ranks to be one of the best.
He was an entrepreneur,
A powerful businessman of sorts,
Shifting people and products
From country to country, port to port.
Dad's confidence was on display
Riding his rumbling bikes.
In his gator attire, he'd hit the streets.
With wind is his hair, he was fast and free.
Dad knew how to work
But also took time to play.
Without a care in the world,
He could fish all day.
Dad's smile filled his face,
And his eyes lit up a room.
He was bold but gentle,
Captivating and smooth.
Dad was a compelling conversationalist,
Brilliantly schooled with mesmerizing facts.

From the streets to the church to politics and sports,
He could respond to nearly anything he was asked.

I stood taller when Daddy was near.
He listened intently, pushing out distractions.
Though he carried strong opinions and convictions.
Whatever I had to say or share,
he was open to listen and ready to hear.
Even laid up in the hospital,
Dad held court until the end.
He was fascinating to the Nurses and Doctors,
As he'd welcome them in as one would a friend.
Just days before he passed,
He said, "Baby, it's okay to cry.
I'm sitting here in my chair
Praying and waiting for my final ride.
Take care of your family,
And finish writing your book,
And please check on Miriam from time to time.
You know I've loved that lady for over half my life."
And as I end this poem, I'll leave you one final message
Dad would want me to say.
I've lived hard and I've lived loud
and I've made many mistakes.
But I've owned them and God knows them
And He loved me just the same.
Pray and love, live bold and be strong.
Remember that Jesus cares,
and that He is near
at just the mention of His name.
Live for God and not man,
And please, by all means, repent of your sins every day.

I referred to my mother in many chapters of this book. Mothers play a powerful role in our lives, whether they are religious, Christians who attend church regularly, prayer warriors who walk in the Spirit, or completely un-churched. No child can truly ever escape a mother's influence. Good, bad, or indifferent, they play a key role in our lives.

My mother brought four children into this world. Each of us saw her in a different light. We all suffered greatly, either at her hand or by her choices. At one point or another, each of us was physically or sexually abused due to Mom's neglect, anger, rage, and pain. Each of us had to wade through the murky waters of our past and accept our upbringing for what it was. Some of us discovered self-destructive vices to numb the pain. Our childhood circumstances led my brother to crime, prison, and ultimately death through an overdose of drugs. Jack spent more time in prison than out of prison. He would get out and try to fight for a normal life, but it never came. He just could not find his way to Christ through the chaos. Wendy became pregnant as a young teen and faced many struggles in life due to the generational curses of addiction that only God can truly break. My sister Vicky struggled for many years, even trying to take her own life, until she fell in love with Jesus Christ through truly studying His Word each day. She even saw a therapist. However, she admits that her true healing came through devouring the Bible. I dabbled with drinking, smoking pot and promiscuity until finding my way to Christ and wholeheartedly saying, "Where He leads me, I will follow." I had to take up my cross and follow Him. I had nothing to offer Jesus but brokenness, pain, and shame, but He had everything to offer me. I had no thoughts for tomorrow. I knew not where I would live, what I would eat, or how I would get through college, but each and every day, He provided the manna I needed until the new day dawned. I learned to completely rely on His promises and trust Him. Mom would disappear for days. I would be home alone, spending hours at a time in prayer. I was scared, but I always had the church as a safe haven. Those early days taught me so much about prayer, fasting, and a prayer-answering God.

When I was in Bible School, I requested prayer for Mom every single day in chapel service. As soon as requests went forth, my arm went up. Everyone knew what I was going to say. They could recite my prayers. I did not care. I had to say it over and over, day after day, month after month, year after year. I asked that group of Bible College friends to pray for my unsaved mother. Every day, I pleaded with God to deliver her soul from bondage. I had seen God deliver many from their history of agony in sin, but ten years later, God allowed me to witness to my mom. My prayer was about to be answered.

Moving to Tupelo Children's Mansion from St. Louis, took me an even greater distance from Mom, who was residing in the Chicago Suburbs. I would call her often and let her know how things were going at the Mansion. With every call, she began to soften and become more open toward the Lord. During this time, I was involved with the Christian Intervention Program and told Mom that we would be heading to Southern Illinois for prison-ministry training. This was only a five-hour drive from Chicago. She told me she was going to come and visit me. I wanted to believe her, but my faith was weak. She didn't always come through on her promises, so I wasn't sure if she would this time either. Terri and I prayed, and God honored our prayers.

Mom stayed true to her promise and came with me to a special church service being held for all the trainees. I don't remember who preached, but as he did, tears began to stream from Mom's eyes and down her face. She wept and prayed, and asked me if she could be baptized! Bro. William Dillon, who coordinated and supervised the training trip, baptized Mom in the name of Jesus, that night! Years of prayers were answered. It was the start of many positive changes in Mom's life. I could instantly see God working in her life. It was a beautiful new beginning for Mom. I had been talking to her for years about Christ while living my faith. Finally, after the loss of my step-father to cancer, Mom let down her guard and wanted God to move in. She was a bit nervous and afraid, but ready and willing for a change, tired of the life she had lived. I count it a joy to have witnessed my mom be cleansed from a past of pain and shame.

Mom moved to Mississippi and worked as a volunteer at the Tupelo Children's Mansion Thrift Store for a season of time. She stayed with me about a year before moving to Florida and then back to Illinois.

My son Landon was born on December 9, 2002. At the time of his birth, Mom came. She stayed with me for several weeks. She cooked for us, and her presence was welcomed and

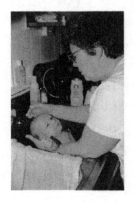

enjoyed. When Landon was four months old, Mom was heading back to Tupelo for a visit when she decided to stop in Ohio and visit Vicky, before continuing her trip. While there, I got a call stating that Mom was very sick, and we needed to come quickly. We drove all night. When we arrived at the hospital, the oncologist informed us that Mom had stage-four lung

159

cancer and only had a short time to live. This was in late July, and she died one month later, on August 27th. I thought about how strenuous it must have been for her to come and care for me during Landon's birth. She appeared weak, but she never gave any indication that she was sick.

I spent those few weeks with her following her diagnosis. She was transferred back to Illinois and was in and out of the hospital. Several of my close friends came to visit her, and I was grateful. A minister by the name of Jack  Yonts, went every day for a week and prayed with Mom. He prayed fervent prayers and read scripture to her. Then the call came. I answered the phone, "Hello?"

Responding he said, "This is Pastor Yonts. I'm here at the hospital, and I thought you would want to hear something. He then put the phone up to my mom, and I could hear her crying out to God, speaking in a heavenly language! It was the miracle for which I had prayed over the past twelve years! God, once again came through!

At her funeral, many people shared with me how my mother's life and testimony had made a difference in theirs. Even though it took her entire life for her to completely understand God's resurrecting power, she had spent the last few years seeking for redemption and helping others in her own way. In fact, my mom was an avid reader and had hundreds of books. She donated many of them to the local prison after reading them and helped to make a difference in many people's lives.

Letter from Mom

On August 12, 2000, Mom penned a letter addressed to no one. Maybe it was a letter to God. Maybe she wrote it hoping her children would one day read it. And, read it we did. I wish I could have read it before she passed away from a fast battle with cancer that took her life just one month after we got word that she was sick. I wish I could have read her words and processed her pain with her. I wish she would have felt safe enough with me to talk through her early years of prostitution, crime, pain, and shame. I wish I could say that nineteen years ago I would have had the wisdom to handle the full truth, and the ability to help Mom grasp true forgiveness. Unfortunately, I'm not sure that I did. Mom was baptized in Jesus name. She was filled with God's Spirit. She lived in repentance, though I'm not completely sure she understood the power of true forgiveness. In her own way, she made peace with each of her children. In our own ways, we each took the shattered pieces of our childhood remains and tried to rebuild. This was easier for some of us because of our commitment to an everlasting Father whose grace is new every day. For my brother Jack, this was not the case. His story ended in despair, and that pain remains present as I write this book. Here are the words she wrote on that summer day over a decade ago.

"I can't talk to people because I have no goals, no dreams, and most of all no talents to pursue. I'm most often intimidated and no longer know how to pursue friendship, so I spend my time alone, because I feel safe. I am reclusive because I feel like a failure. I know as I look back on my life, I've been too stupid to even learn from my own mistakes. When I was very young, I was happy and knew how to unconditionally love, but once my eyes were opened to the real world, I felt betrayed and I could no longer live that.

I feel like a stupid fool going down one bad road after another. I don't want to make a mistake or disappoint anyone anymore or be an embarrassment to God or my family. Without talent or trained skills, I can't really make a difference. Have you ever felt unworthy? I've run out of energy and self-confidence. I've never been a leader only a follower. Now that my husband has passed, I have no one to follow and most of the time I don't feel like God can hear me. I try to strengthen my faith each day, but I don't know how to do this either. I know being a good person isn't good enough. I need to be hard working, loving, positive, caring, giving, faithful, honest, and I'm none of these things.

I'm hurt, lonely, angry, bitter, and discouraged. I'm ashamed of my past and my present. I started out being a good mother, but I made some very bad choices and ended up as a failure. And yes, I live with the guilt, disgrace and shame. The wrongdoings in my past are unforgiveable. I've stolen; I've lied; I've cheated. I've had wrongful associations and done dishonest acts against others and myself. I've been disloyal to mankind and disobedient to God. I'm a disgrace to the human race. I'm a disgrace to God. I write these truths for healing, but I still don't know how to look forward and make something of myself.

I don't go for help because I can't talk to people without tears. I'm tired of crying and ashamed that tears are my only emotion these days. My life needs purpose. I'm always running, and I'm tired. I just don't know how to open myself up to God. Sometimes I think I have. I want to share these things so that I can feel His presence, but I never do. I want to hear Him speak to me.

I've spent my entire life on the run. I run, but I no longer know where to go. The truth is, it's not about where I live. It's never been about a place. It's not about currently deciding between Illinois, Mississippi or Florida. It's about the lack of belonging. Since losing my husband, I am an unnecessary burden to everyone.

I know that my unhappiness and guilt I carry was all created by me. I realize that all of my problems and heartaches have been due to a lifetime of bad choices. I've put these feelings on paper and realize that they are now out there. If anyone one day reads this, please know if I've caused you any hurt or pain in your life, please forgive me."

My Heartfelt Prayer

As Mom so aptly penned the words in her song, "I was born among hard times." I always had my goals set high, and though she did not personally teach me, I did indeed learn how to pray. Over twenty schools later, many states, horrific recollections of abuse, abandonment, and neglect - these all led me to that old fashioned altar where I met the Creator of the universe and Healer of my soul. Then, in the form of real people, Jesus appeared at my job and spoke to me as a teenage girl. He prompted me to follow Him at all costs. He healed me of scars, pain and shame, almost instantly. He called me for training and equipped me for service. He enlarged my territory and blessed me with a wonderful husband, three beautiful children, and three darling grandchildren. He has continued to hold my hand through great adversities. I have trusted Him through the trials. He has never left me or forsaken me. He is my refuge, my present help in the time of trouble.

It wasn't easy to pen my story, but my prayer is that it brings you hope. My prayer is for you to know that Jesus loves the dirty, the broken, and the unjust. My prayer is that this book will ignite the church-going teenager to light their world and witness to someone to whom nobody else can relate. My prayer is that the Bible Quizzer who reads this will accept the call on their life, and though you may face adversities, go wherever God leads. My prayer is for the unmarried to trust God with their heart and trust His timing. My prayer is for moms and dads to pick up their *Sword* and bring God back into their homes. My prayer is that Christians would live out their faith, living according to the Word and loving others, even as Christ loves us. We will be hurt. We will get sick. Our marriages will face deep valleys. Our ministries will be tried. Our character will be tested. We will be hurt by friends, co-workers and family. The truth of the matter is, people hurt people. Hurt will choose you. It has chosen me many times throughout the years. But, I have also chosen not to allow it to have a hold on me! I did not get to choose my parents. Neither did you. I did not get to choose my pain. I'm sure you didn't either. However, we can choose to live at the foot of the cross so forgiveness comes easy and healing can flow. Jesus loves you my friend! Cry out to Him so He can heal your hurts and set you free!

I was hurt…

…He healed me!

I was hungry for Him…

…He anointed me!

I was willing…

…He equipped me!

I was equipped…

…He appointed me!

I've been appointed…

…and He's kept me!

He can keep you too!

My early life trained me to run the race I am running today. God always has a master plan. We simply have to trust the way-maker.

Conclusion

Our childhood years go with us for a lifetime. So much of what transpires during that formative time period follows us into adulthood. For some, those years become a crutch or a chain about their necks. As you read in the above chapters, I determined not to allow the pain caused by others to define me as an adult. God healed me. He transformed my life. At the time of this writing, I am celebrating over 25 years of working in ministry at Tupelo Children's Mansion. The hurts chosen for me as a child, have become my ministry. I am not a licensed counselor, but God has ordained my path, enabling me to minister to hundreds of children over the past two decades. I am not yet a licensed minister, yet the Lord has anointed me to preach the truth of the Gospel when asked by my pastor. I received my teaching degree, but I do not daily teach in a classroom setting. I give instruction in photography and Bible Quizzing, and I often conduct chapel services. I love to help others.

Thankful and grateful for my wonderful husband, I love and appreciate him, and the beautiful, crazy, winding roads that we have already traveled together on this journey of life. We have had many bumps along the way. We have struggled just like any other couple; nevertheless, God has never once failed us. Marriage, in our case, has defied the odds thus far, even though statistically, there was a good chance for failure. When two people from broken backgrounds create a bond through the sanctity of marriage, it often produces a future broken couple. This is not our case. It isn't because we are special or lucky. Our marriage is work, just like every other couple who has said, "I am here through the good, the bad, and the tough times!" My husband is everything a husband should be to me, and I try to be everything a wife should be to him.

I love being a mother to our beautiful children and first class son-in-law. All three of our children have been a joy to raise. They love God, and it shows in their character and actions. I'm *mimi* to our beautiful grandbabies, and they light my world!

In business, I have been blessed to lead a large group of Scentsy consultants. At the time of this writing, we have several hundred on our team and nearly one-thousand men and women in our entire down-line. The business of direct sales work with this company, has been a blessing in our lives. Our team is our family. Our friends.

I serve Tupelo Children's Mansion as the Director of Sponsor Relations. Sharing my passion for this God-ordained ministry is something which still excites me. My *job* never feels like work, because I love what I do! I enjoy connecting our sponsors and children. I'm happy assisting Pastor and Sister Judd in any way that I can, whether it be writing, photography, fundraising, or speaking in church and conferences. They have been my leaders for nearly two decades, and they have led our staff in creating a culture of camaraderie and loyalty on the Mansion campus. This is important to me.

My own early years of Bible Quizzing have stayed with me. I serve as the Bible Quizzing Coordinator at the Mansion and have coached teams for many years. I know how much this ministry changed my life, and I am overjoyed to see it transform the lives of others, including my own children's. Bible Quizzing is a huge part of our campus. Through commitment to scripture memorization and planting the Word of God in their hearts, young people develop maturity in their minds, attitudes, and emotions. Socialization skills are increased because of competition with other church-going youths. They learn the importance of living a Christian life, growing spiritually. It is an honor to see how this program molds, shapes and changes the course of history in young people's lives. We love this program and are thankful for the leadership of Tim and Jennifer Matthews, our close friends and leaders, who have helped us develop this strong ministry on our campus.

I wear a lot of hats, and more than anything, my goal each day is to be a Christian, no matter which hat I'm wearing. I want to be Christ-like in everything I do and say. Hurt chose me as a child and has visited many times along life's journey, but I strive to keep it from becoming a permanent resident within my heart. To accomplish this, I pray each day for a clean heart despite any unpleasant offenses or circumstances that arise.

God took my life, the brokenness, pain, shame, and hurt, and He used those circumstances to mold me into the woman of God He desired. I did not know about prayer when I stared aimlessly out the window of that Chevy van all those years ago, although somehow I knew I was called to be a light and share hope. I wrote this book for that very reason. We all have a story. Yours may be different, better, easier, or harder, worse, and more trying than mine. It does not matter. What matters is your choice in how you allow your circumstances to shape and dictate your life. If you choose God, you are making a decision to let God frame your life according to His will. Don't hide or be ashamed of your story. Own it. Embrace it! Allow it to mold and shape you. Take your hurts to the Lord and He can heal you! Take your healing and allow it to help others. Just because hurt chose you, does not mean it gets to control you! He can take your brokenness and make you whole. He can take your tests and make them your testimony!

Tupelo Children's Mansion
From Behind My Lens

The sunlight peeks through the trees, gently kissing the newly designed fall backdrop featuring a winding, paved driveway. I'm waiting for my first student wanderer to step into the colorful scenery of my photography world. From behind my lens, I will use my photographer's paintbrush to capture the beauty of the child.

Memory cards, fresh batteries, reflectors, and a large drink all sit on a table close by, as my assistants and I eagerly greet our first little subject. It is picture day for the Tupelo Children's Mansion children as well as those who attend our on-campus Christian school. However, for us, it's so much more than a photograph.

Each child is a real person, maneuvering through life, discovering their purpose, and finding their calling, while realizing their own self-worth. Knowing this, it's an amazing opportunity for me to reach beyond the snap of a camera-button and sincerely work to create an image that is beautiful. We strive to make each child feel confident and comfortable in our presence, and alleviate their fear of the camera. Aperture, shutter speed, lines, and light mean everything in a portrait, but as the artist, I don't ever want to forget that the focus of my artistry is a real person.

So many times, I have gently touched the face of a child, and I can see the loneliness and pain they try so desperately to hide. At that moment, it is my prayer to minister through the lens by helping to depict the beauty that lies within that soul, as if to offer a promise for better days ahead.

After the processing of portraits, I will see teens walk a little taller, a smile on their faces, as they eagerly share their prints with their teachers and peers. Only a photographer knows the amount of work that goes into true portraiture, but the final masterpiece is always worth the journey it required to get there.

I am thankful I was handed the camera on that first day I arrived at the Mansion because it has become another major part of who I am. Through the years, I have learned the art of professional photography, and I take my art seriously. It's not just snapping a picture to me. The world, especially my Mansion world, is the canvas I see from behind my lens as I photograph every aspect of life at TCM (Tupelo Children's Mansion). This chapter had to be included to give you a glimpse into this window of my life that means so much to me.

Just yesterday, a young lady gave me the impression that she was ugly, awkward, and uncomfortable with pictures. A few moments later, after being sat among the fall leaves, with the dance of sunlight across her back, and a few kind words of

affirmation and reassurance, she smiled at me as I showed her a portrait of a beautiful young lady, in a whole new light. It is for those instants that I pray will happen again and again, as I paint from behind my lens.

A portion of the proceeds from the sales of this book benefits the children who call TCM their home. Tupelo Children's Mansion (TCM) is a residential group home serving families and children in crisis situations. Founded in 1953, in Tupelo, Mississippi, the Mansion has provided temporary or long-term care to hundreds of children needing a safe and loving environment. It is recognized as one of the finest and most trusted institutions of its kind.

To find out more about the Tupelo Children's Mansion, go to www.mansionkids.org.

Made in the USA
Coppell, TX
21 May 2020

25194934R00095